MOTHERHOOD ON THE LINE

When my automatic dryer died I thought I would too.

Lee told me he thought it was a blessing in disguise. He said in this day and age people were far too mechanically minded anyway and he went right out and bought me a clothesline. Not only would a clothesline save electricity and money, he said, but our clothes would smell better, the exercise would do me good and I'd feel alive and more like getting my work done. "Wanta' bet?" I felt like saying but instead I acted thrilled and said "Thank you, there is nothing I wanted more than a clothesline. Never mind that I don't own pearls, mink, diamonds or an automatic dryer. A clothesline is much, much better." He was pleased that I liked it.

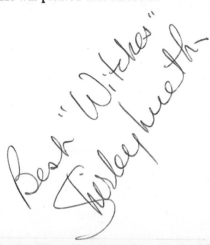

Best "Witches"
Lesley Smeth

I DIDN'T PLAN TO BE A WITCH

SHIRLEY LUETH

I Didn't Plan To Be A Witch

By Shirley Lueth

Copyright© 1981 by Shirley Lueth
This Edition Originally Published by
AVON BOOKS
A division of
The Hearst Corporation
Original ISBN 0-380-77875-0
Now Published by Lueth House Publishing Co.
1409 9th St. – Aurora, NE 68818
NEW ISBN 0-937911-02-X

First Lueth House Printing June 1988

To my husband, Lee, and the prayer-and-peanut-butter gang . . . this is your book. Thank you for letting me write it.

Table of Contents

SECTION IV

THERE GOES MY OPINIONS, MY MONEY, MY PEACE OF MIND, AND MY CAR

Senior High Stage

SECTION V

IF GOD HAD WANTED THEM TO GO TO COLLEGE, HE WOULD HAVE PAID THEIR TUITION

College-Age Stage

SECTION VI

THE FAMILY TREE GROWS AND GROWS

Married Child Stage

SECTION VII
GRANDMA WILL YOU BABY-SIT? NOT TONIGHT, THANK YOU
Grandchild Stage

GRANDMA WILL YOU, BABY-SIT
BUT YOU'RE TERRIBLE YOU

Grand with Son

Foreword

There was a time when I considered myself a cheerful, pleasant, polite, and gracious person. Then I became a mother and gradually the process of developing a rotten disposition set in. My voice, once thought to be low and sensuous, has acquired the tone of Attila the Hun.

I didn't plan to be a witch . . . it just worked out that way.

I have gone through various stages of Witchydom these past twenty-eight years. Currently I am covering only five of the seven possibilities: junior high, senior high, college, married child, and "Grandma, will you baby-sit? Not tonight, thank you" stage. The other two stages, infant through preschool and kindergarten through sixth grade, are carved in my memory. I have total recall and instant cold chills.

I think I've become a professional witch. I know the gratifications and grumblings of being a mother. I have touched on the good, the bad, and the evil of all seven stages. Add my husband, Lee, and our pet, Augie-Doggie, and I can peek into nearly every family home in the United States. Maybe even the world. Maybe even yours.

I have been the type of mother who often wished she was a princess. I have craved complete isolation from detergent boxes, tinker toys, and pairs of raveled undershorts . . . sizes four and forty-two. And I often say so . . . out loud. I alibi my way to sleep at night by asking Whoever Is Up There Listening to forgive me for being such a cross, lousy mother so often during the day and then I promise, on my honor, that tomorrow I will do better and then I wake up in the morning and find that someone dumped all the expensive chocolate chips in the dog's dish and it starts all over again.

Some days I am a better witch than I am others. Some days I am quite nice.

Some days I feel blessed (and amazed) that John, now a productive and professional insurance salesman in Chi-

11

cago, Illinois, is the same young man who used to peer up the dresses of mannikins in large, expensive department stores. When he was four years old.

That our oldest daughter Karen had the good sense to pick out our son-in-law.

That twenty-three-year-old David, who counts a soccer ball and waterbed as his most prized possessions, still has manners enough to stand up when his aunt enters a room.

That an independent, grown-up Susan calls often and says, "I'm lonely. I want to come home."

Mary just comes home, without calling, which proves she's not as independent and grown-up as she thought.

Amy wants to go into journalism because Mom has such fun sitting hunched sweating, smoking, and swearing over her typewriter.

And Claudia, the youngest child. Oh, that Claudia. She's straightforward in speech, action, and desire, and almost always calls home to let us know where she is.

As for my husband and the dog, both keep me warm at night, and who could ask for more?

I didn't plan to be an angel, either . . . and it hardly ever works out that way. Only at Christmas and on Mother's Day, when it really counts.

It has not been easy for my family, living with a witch. Especially a witch that writes. While most mommies smelled of talcum powder and freshly baked cookies, my children came home to a mommy who wore floppy bedroom slippers, tucked a pencil in her hair, had a scowl on her face, and smelled of carbon paper and typewriter ribbons. My husband didn't know when he came home from work whether dinner was going to be ragout or rejection slips.

But they've been good sports and they've given me the best years of my life. Of course, I wouldn't want to come right out and tell them this . . . Even a mother needs her secret thoughts.

SECTION I

PAMPERS AND PEANUT BUTTER

Infant and Preschool Stage

My God, Someone's Smearing Shortening on the Cat

I wish I could say that during my first pregnancy I shot out of bed each morning, played a game of golf, jogged four miles, drank gallons of cold milk, took my vitamins regularly, and didn't show until the seventh month. No. I ballooned five minutes after conception and crept about the house suffering from nausea, splotchy skin, and a very bad attitude. I also had a sour stomach. My mother told me this was to be expected. She said indigestion and heartburn meant the baby had a lot of hair. "Good Lord," I told my husband, Lee. "This child will come into the world with hair down to its kneecaps." He told me not to worry. He told me that it was only an old wive's tale and went back to sleep. I sat, propped up by four pillows, and spent the night wondering what we would name a fuzzy baby. I also wondered what I would do with a baby, fuzzy or not.

I did not want to admit to my almost embarrassingly new husband that I knew very little about babies. Heavens, he was still in shock from learning that I did not know how to cook or clean. His mother pursed her lips and shook her head when we announced our wedding plans and mine turned white around the eyes and gnawed her knuckles. My dad laughed right out loud. Now, here I was expecting a baby and the flowers were still fresh from the wedding. I am sure that when my husband said "I do" he did not intend to do *it* all at once. Nevertheless, we were having a baby, and though we didn't know it, we were starting a chain reaction, and would devote the next two or three hundred years of our married life to raising children.

When Karen was born I was thrilled to find she had a normal amount of soft, brown hair. Other things disappointed me. I had thought that dressing her would be like dressing a dolly. I had not thought any baby (especially mine) would pucker her tiny rosebud mouth and spit sour milk on me. I had thought she would fall asleep upon being placed in a clean, pink-sheeted crib, and that shadowy angels would sit upon the night light and handle emergencies. How surprised I was when I discovered the only person whose hands were going to be called into service were my own. And I was no angel. Not at 2:30 a.m.

"The baby is crying." I poked Lee. My eyes were stuck shut and I was sure my labor pains were returning. We had brought Karen home from the hospital twenty-four hours ago and she had slept only thirty minutes of that time.

"Sure enough," Lee mumbled in his sleep. "That's nice." He was not being cold and hard-hearted. He was not being a bad daddy. He was just tired. Very tired. His entire life style had changed in one short, triumphant severing of an umbilical cord. So had mine. I knew I should approach motherhood naturally. I knew that if it was accepted in the proper relaxed manner it would be terrific. Yet, I kept making mistakes and harboring misconceptions. But I did not become disillusioned. I continued to be a pushover for a tiny anything . . . a kitten, a piglet, a baby goat, or goldfish. It didn't matter. If it was little and helpless, my instincts soared. I immediately wanted to take care of it. Age has not lessened those instincts—just my stomach muscles. True, the instincts have sputtered and crash-landed on occasion, but I am thankful to say I never did lose my ability to react positively to babies and it's a good thing. Karen was five months old when I became pregnant again.

"Wow!" Lee said with a surprised look on his face. "It sure happens quick, doesn't it!

Susan moved into the room with Karen and learned at once to dodge the alphabet blocks, plastic rattles, baby shoes, and hardbacked books that were tossed into her crib while she was sleeping by an older sister who wasn't so old herself. For someone who knew nothing about babies, I learned fast. And faster and faster—for following Karen and Susan came

John, David, Mary, Amy, and Claudia. Each a special birth, each a special pleasure, and each a special surprise. A surprise to me, to Lee, to the doctor, to family and friends. Telling other people that I was expecting another baby . . . and another . . . and another . . . and another was one of the things that bothered me most. Lee tried to convince me that this attitude was silly. After all, he didn't mind and the doctor didn't mind and the children we already had didn't care. "As long as we love them, feed them, and clothe them," he persuaded, patting me on the head, "what difference does one more make?" Now that they are growing up and asking for tuition money I'm not so sure he thinks we were so smart. I knew some people regarded me as either a sex maniac or a simpleton, but I really and truly thought if I could raise one, I could raise seven.

I got up every morning and tried very hard to keep the children from poking apple cores down the plumbing or eating the toilet paper or throwing baloney on the floor or tearing houseplants up by the roots or putting beans in their ears. Each day I simply swept up the wreckage and wondered if I would outlive the broom.

I did not have a schedule, a plan of attack, or a routine. All I had was determination to get through the day. One second at a time. If I survived until noon I felt lucky. If dinnertime came and went without my caving in completely, it was cause for celebration. Bedtime brought with it the happy realization that I had endured. I didn't quibble with the Lord during nightly prayers. I simply said . . . "Thank You."

There was no such thing as A Minute To Myself. I took a bath with the door open, the faucets quiet, kept the soap out of my ears in order to hear who was stuffing dominoes in the current baby's mouth, who had crawled up onto the kitchen cabinets to ravish the marshmallows, who was calling Grandmother long distance, who was unscrewing the screen door, or who was piddling in Daddy's pineapple plant. Years went by before I felt confident enough to lock the bathroom door and luxuriate in good, hot, bubbly water. Even today, if I'm bathing and hear a cupboard creak, I think, "My God, someone is smearing shortening on the cat!"

I lived under a great many misconceptions during those days. I remember gazing down with pride on Karen in her bassinet and whispering to Lee, "I can't wait until she learns to crawl!" What a silly thing to say.

Lee thought it was nice that she stayed put in one place long enough for us to have an uninterrupted meal. He was the smart one in the family. He still is. I had foolishly believed the dictionary definition of the word crawl . . . "To move slowly across the ground, as a worm . . . to advance timorously and slyly." I didn't realize that any kid worth a soaked Pamper, after learning the proper moves, can outrun any thoroughbred in the country. Crawl, indeed. "Presto" would be more like it. "Presto" she was near the hot stove. "Presto" she was behind the couch. "Presto" the door of the closet slammed on her fingers. "Presto" she had eaten a cigarette. "Presto" she had followed the dog outside. For the life of me I couldn't figure why they used the word "crawl."

I thought I could sit her up when she was eight months old and surround her with squeaky toys and plastic doodads and turn my back. Oh, I knew she might creep a few inches to reach a favorite bunny rabbit, but I had no idea that I would be crawling after her around the clock. Of course, Lee was there, but he was not tuned in. He didn't even react when an African violet thudded to the carpet. He didn't take his forehead from the sports page when Karen screamed because she was hung up in the rungs of the dining room chair. He was not aware that Augie-Doggie's eyes were popping out of his head in terror because someone was chewing on his tail. It was only when the front page of the newspaper leisurely made its crumpled way across the room that he became conscious of the fact that a demon lived in our house.

Along about David I learned the futility of bathing a crawling child. It was a waste of time, unless he went directly from bath to bed. It was not fair to measure my housekeeping abilities with his fingernails. David was born with dirt magnets on his elbows and knees. He could find it anywhere. Let me wash the kitchen floor and he found a dead box elder bug and ate it. Put down an orange long enough to spit out a seed and he had rubbed it in his hair. When I put garbage in a sack, you-know-who gnawed a hole in it and smacked his lips over the coffee grounds. Librarians of all ages and dispositions begged me not to continue to bring back borrowed books that had been licked. I desperately asked them to take David in exchange for the mutilated book.

Karen and Susan were not pleased to have been provided with a second crawling brother. John had been a novelty and therefore tolerated, but enough was enough. They kept reminding me how awful it was. "Mom!" the after-school cry echoed through to the kitchen. "Come get the baby. He's eating my homework again. The teacher doesn't believe me when I tell her my baby brother swallowed my arithmetic." Karen, a very conscientious student, was close to tears. "Why don't you tie him up like you do Augie?" she suggested. "He's like a spider. Now you see him . . . now you don't. All I have to do is take my Barbie clothes out of their box and there he is in my room. I don't have one set of doll shoes left."

I know how she felt. I hadn't seen my car keys in three weeks.

Little moist spots appeared all over our carpeting along with other "droppings" too numerous to mention. I followed the first child armed with clean diapers, talcum powder, and gallons of rug shampoo. As the last made her way around the woodwork, I put four pairs of plastic pants on her and rubbed my foot on the nap in a vain effort to restore the shag in the rug.

Every person in our neighborhood, on our Christmas list, and in both families avoided our house as baby beds stacked up in the corner and high chairs lined the dining room wall. Obviously, I had not mastered motherhood. Mealtime threw me into a domestic dither. Lee arrived home from work at six o'clock in the evening and found me, more likely than not, standing by the stove with a sobbing infant in one arm, a toddler fastened to my knees, and my own tears mingling with the baby's in the broccoli. I seldom had to commercially salt a meal. Furthermore, the rustle of a cookbook and the rattle of a pan set the others off like skyrockets. John teased Karen, someone tied knots in Augie's tail, Susan turned on the television full blast, David twisted the drapes to make sailing ships, and Mary threw up. There was something about the preparation of food that could make this perfectly healthy child spike a temperature of 104° the minute I turned the oven on. It was the low ebb of my day.

Lee couldn't understand why I became so excited when he invited someone from the office home for dinner. "It's not that big a deal," he said. Well, it is when you only have two table knives because all the rest are buried in the back yard. It's tiresome asking guests to share something as intimate as eating utensils. How do you explain the table manners of a two-year-old who picks up her plate and slams it to the floor to announce that she has either finished eating or doesn't like it. Or how do you carry on a gracious conversation when a four-year-old goes "aaack, aaack, aaack" every time you offer peas, and a six-year-old hides mashed potatoes in a napkin, or a dog pants at your elbow for a handout? Possibly I minded it more than the guests.

Often, during those days, I wondered if I would ever have time to put on a clean blouse for dinner, open a bottle of wine for my husband, teach the children some dainty manners, and stop having to eat every meal with one foot in a running position. I learned to feed a baby with one hand, me with the other, and it wasn't until I devoured a can of strained spinach and the baby had swiss steak that I discontinued dual feedings. Oh, I learned, but I didn't always love it.

I did love, however, the tousled little curly head that often spied a Cheerio on the floor while her head was bent in prayer, placing it into a Mary-mouth and peeping over tiny fingers to see if anyone had observed such unforgiveable greed. And I loved the smell of a four-year-old boy, brown as a chestnut from dirt and sweat and suntan, running in from play to go to the bathroom, get a cracker, and see if I was still hanging around the house. And I loved handing over the crown and conceding defeat to a friend with five children under the age of six, who called to say she was having twins in September and what could she do! I said, "Enjoy!" and she answered, "How can I? The baby is sleeping in the utility room now . . . where will I put two more?" I loved not being her.

I learned to quick-bake forty-eight cookies at 3:30 p.m.,

knowing there would only be one left by the time dessert rolled around, and I accepted the fact my husband was able to sleep the moment his head hit the pillow. I learned not to weep because he could sleep while I got up fifteen times throughout the night warming bottles, covering cold bottoms, fetching drinks, finding lost blankets, patting away nightmares, letting the dog out, and worrying about rabies . . . and rabies shots. There had never been a known case of rabies in our area but I worried about what I would do if there was.

And I took great comfort in the fact Lee continued to think I had nice legs even when my stomach popped out.

Baby Angel Lowers the Boom

I took potty-training as seriously as I did childbirth. I couldn't wait to try my hand. I gathered up hundreds of child-care manuals, read them voraciously, and told Lee it was time to potty-train Karen. I knew it would be a meaningful experience for both of us.

"But she's only three weeks old," he said. "Isn't that a little young?"

"You can't start too soon on formative habits," I explained. "The experts say so. We could warp her forever if we wait much longer." Talk about warp! Did you ever try to place a baby whose head still wobbles on the hard fact of an adult toilet seat? "I need help!" I screamed to Lee. "Fast!" He saw right away that I could not hold up both ends of a limp baby at the same time. While I gripped the lower portion, her little head lolled, burying her nose in her stomach and shutting off air passage. When I kept her neck rigidly in place, there was great danger of the bottom half dropping off into the sewer.

"This isn't working," I sobbed frantically, "this isn't working at all. I get muscle cramps and she goes to sleep gasping for breath. I am spending half of my day holed up in a bathroom with a three-week-old and the other half changing and washing dirty diapers. Something is wrong somewhere."

Lee suggested that I might have started too soon. "You must have misread the instructions," he said. I didn't think so. I was sure it said that even a tiny infant would react in a positive manner to the stimulus of bottom adhering to porcelain. I was just having problems getting her bottom to adhere, that's all. She was slippery and slithery and one little foot kept dropping down into the stool and she cried and I cried and Lee finally insisted that I wait until she learned to sit alone. He told me he would buy us a regular potty chair. He said natural instinct ordinarily took care of the mechanics of potty-training. He said that little children were very alert to their environment. That they learned by example. He said that as soon as she observed the fact that her mother and father did not wear diapers she would understand the whole thing. I guess he was right. Karen is twenty-seven years old and hasn't worn a diaper in years.

Even with my good intentions, our children were the slowest tinkle on the block. Coffee klatches found me burying my nose in the draperies, trying to hide when the subject of potty-training came up. It was obvious there wasn't another woman in the room whose child wet its panties after the age of one. How I longed to hear someone say, "Well, I packed Joey's Pampers and peanut butter sandwiches and sent him off to camp today."

It wasn't that our children were slow-witted or anything. It's just that some were more gracious about it than others. Some were downright stubborn. I told Lee I couldn't show the boys how to do it properly. "I didn't have the benefit of a tutor," he said, "and I see no reason why I should hold court in the bathroom for a bunch of little boys." The one time he consented, John brought in three friends from across the street and two from down the block. One of them was a girl. It was the talk of the neighborhood for six weeks and one of the mothers tried to start a rumor that the Lueth house was certainly not a proper atmosphere for other children. Lee was embarrassed and I thought it was funny.

David did everything to stave off the day when he could discard his diaper. He hid the potty under his bed, put the deflector in the oven, turned the chair upside down, and placed towels over it, hoping to disguise it completely. He even volunteered to fold his own laundry, hoping to ease my work load. "It's like death and taxes, kiddo," I told him as he dragged his feet all the way down the hallway to the bathroom. "You gotta' do it!" He pitched a fit and I gave him a cookie. It worked. The solution to potty-training came out of a cookie jar. Every time David accomplished what he was supposed to accomplish I handed him a cookie. We had it down to a science. And we did it so well that no one else in the family caught on. It was our little secret until I wrote this book.

We had gone through all the normal euphemisms used to denote the bathroom and "tee-tee" had been a favorite. Lee thought I should find something else when the boys were little because "tee-tee" sounded effeminate. "We're going to have to decide on something, soon," I said. "When John has to go to the bathroom he stands there, shuffles his feet, and turns red in the face. He looks like he is having a heart attack. It scares his grandmother." Lee told me to take him in, point it out, give it a name, and stick with it. "There's no real reason why he can't learn the proper terminology." I listed the common nouns and adjectives ordinarily used in conjunction with bathroom activities. Some of them I said out loud . . . some I mouthed. "Do you really want an innocent child talking like a drunken sailor?" I asked. I thought this could prove more uncomfortable than his still wearing diapers.

Lee thought it over and suggested that I find something John could identify with. "Something masculine, something male," he said, "and then repeat, repeat, repeat. He'll catch on." John was bright and wanted desperately to please me, but when you don't know what to call something you can't very well do it justice.

"That's dandy," I said in a husky voice twenty-three times a day, as I propelled John into the bathroom, "a real dandy! You are a fine cowboy!" Cowboy-dandies were born and lived in our household for many years. It was a good code, but I became terribly tired of explaining it to teachers.

By the time Claudia was born I was very bored with tee-tees and cowboy-dandies and discussing it and becoming enthusiastic about it or even worrying about it. "I suppose it is time I trained Claudia," I yawned as I held her up for her daddy to admire. "She's three years old," Lee said. "It might be too late. Maybe she missed out on the basics."

"Oh, she can learn," I assured him. "She's a quick study." I had no doubt that she would learn in a hurry if someone would just take the time to explain it to her. Heavens, she could ride a tricycle like a professional, color within the lines, recite "Humpty Dumpty" faultlessly, and name all the Muppets on Sesame Street. She had the ability. But I had thrown the potty chair away. "Remember?" I reminded Lee. "You told me to get rid of all that damn stuff." The two of us had concluded that we were through having babies. I had also thrown, or given away, the high chair, the infant seat, the sterilizer, the car seat, and all the baby clothes.

So we bought another potty chair and overnight Claudia caught on. I knew she would. She loved that little chair. She sat on it to watch television, to eat her breakfast, and to entertain guests. She spent so much time sitting there she learned its original purpose by osmosis. She didn't give up her little chair until she entered kindergarten. It was the only thing she didn't have to share with a group.

Obviously, potty sessions took a good deal of my time during the preschool years and I thanked God every day for the invention of the automatic washer and dryer. If I didn't know what to do with something I simply washed it. And with the mountains of diapers, training pants, and undershorts that I fed it every day, in addition to sheets, pillowcases, blouses, towels, slacks, dresses, rags, rugs, bones, bottles, and beer caps, the poor washing machine chewed and spit out semiwhite and faded colors like a sausage grinder. I seldom gave it a chance to behave in a dainty manner, and its exclusive cycles such as "presoak," "delicate" and "wrinkles-out" stood idle as I turned on "hard wash" and let her rip. David stood on a small step stool and threw newspapers in the "gick-gock" to watch them shred, and Mary bathed the family cat with a load of Lee's good shirts. The repair man became an intimate family friend. He spent more time at our house than he did his own. We went through a great number of washers and dryers during the first years of our marriage, and almost twice as many plastic pools.

I suppose in the past twenty-odd years we have spent enough on cheap, limp, plastic pools to have comfortably installed and paid for one regulation, Olympic-sized kidney-shaped permanent Hollywood-type swimming pool, complete with filter system, water temperature control, diving board, patio tables, colorful cabana, and a privacy fence. A pool was never used more than one summer. By the middle of August it had lost its fat, plump-air look, and the kids were complaining that every time they sat on it the water ran out over the edges and what was left eventually leaked from the tiny puncture holes that ran up and down the sides. I told them if they hadn't allowed Augie-Doggie to bomb around in it like a Hairy Jaws they might have an even-up chance of having a pool that lasted until school started.

Every summer morning I threatened the children with the you-can't-go-swimming-if-you-don't-be-good routine, and every summer morning they knew I was only fooling. They knew that as soon as nap time ended, along about two, I would break down and let them swim. They knew because they had watched while I blew up the pool, hanging out of their windows and cheering as my face swelled and my eyes popped out. They thought watching was almost as much fun as swimming. Lee warned me not to leave yellowish-brown fairy rings in the lawn because I didn't move the pool enough, and Auntie-dear threw up her hands and said that she certainly hoped I knew better than to put it in the front where the neighbors could see. In her day, she said, little children did chores in the afternoon—like harvest corn, pick apples, and pluck chickens. Swimming meant a creek in the back of the woods once a week to get clean. I told her times had changed.

Auntie-dear lived two hundred miles away, visited once ever three or four months, still wore Blue Waltz perfume, brought expensive presents at Christmas time, and had not chick nor child of her very own. She was a child expert who refused to baby-sit. I loved her. And because she was my relative and Lee loved me, he tolerated her. Barely. She had helped raise me. "Mark my words, Wanda," she told my mother, "if Shirley continues to turn cartwheels, play baseball, climb trees, and shoot marbles, she will suffer later. She will dearly pay for it. She will never be able to have Children!" That was a laugh.

Every summer I visualized the perfect set-up. Every summer I visualized settling into a shaded reclining lawn chair—close enough to the pool to keep an eye out but far enough away not to be splashed—a cool drink in one hand, a hot book in the other, and a transistor radio by my side to mute the sounds of happy childen at play. It never happened that way. As I prepared to take my first sip and reread a particularly satisfying and descriptive paragraph, David would pick that moment to hold Mary's head under water. I lectured him on sibling murder and banished him to the house to drip on his bedroom carpet, handing Mary a plastic duck and restoring peace for two and a half minutes. This gave me enough time to read "He looked at her with excited eyes . . ." when Amy swallowed too much water, gagged, and threw up in the pool, making everyone else sick to their stomachs and making it necessary for me to get up out of my chair, move the pool and my chair to another spot, and refill the pool. Now I was as hot as the characters in the book and the ice had melted in my drink. Susan pulled the plug, as a funny joke, and all the fresh water drained out. Screams of frustration whipped through the neighborhood and everyone threatened to bong her on the head with a toy sprinkling can. I was tempted to let them bong away, but I knew I could not do that. I was a good mother. Besides, how could I have explained to their father? Wearily, I got up, moved the pool and my chair and filled 'er up again. I picked up my book, sighed sensuously, and savored a four-letter word that made my eyes look like they did when I blew up the pool and I heard the call . . .

"Mommy!"

"God, what now!" I thought, and looked in the direction of the swimming pool. Five children had vacated the pool and were standing beside it holding their noses and pointing at Claudia. She was totally ignoring them, sitting placidly and happily pitty-pattying the water with innocent hands. She had forgotten that she had been potty-trained in all the excitement. Augie took it upon himself to walk away in distasteful dignity and lie in my lawn chair. As I lifted Claudia carefully from the pool, carried her inside, and picked up the Chlorox to take back out to scour and disinfect the pool, I made a vow not to compare the fictional heroine's summer activities with my own. I couldn't anyway . . . because there's no way I could liken passionate pettings with poopy pools.

3

Don't Fence Me In

I don't know how anyone can raise a child without a fence. You'd almost think God would send pickets with them when they were born. Before we had one I chased little children in and out of our house all day long, trying to keep them out of the road and away from harm. The minute Karen was tall enough to unlock the screen door she became the Abraham Lincoln of our household; she freed the slaves every fifteen minutes. I didn't blame them, for I didn't like having to stay inside with the dirty dishes, either, but until they were old enough to give out their name, address, and Dad's telephone extension at work, I didn't want them running around willy-nilly without supervision. Augie-Doggie was required, by law, to stay at home, and I thought it best to keep everyone under school age in the yard, too. I needed to know they were safe and within hugging distance. Therefore, as soon as the current baby graduated from the bars of the play-pen, he or she was placed behind the rails of a fence. The first five years of their lives were seen through horizontal lines of some kind.

Our first fence was made of a series of limp chicken wire held together with spit and staples. I stood in the doorway of our house and thought the entire yard looked like a concentration camp. All it lacked was barbed wire across the top. At the edge of each fence post I planted gladiola bulbs upside down and waited for them to grow. When they didn't, I cried because the whole thing was so ugly and ungainly, and Lee wiped my eyes and promised to build a better white wooden one just like they had in storybooks. "Build it strong," I told him, standing

29

Shirley Lueth

back to let him carry the first load of lumber from the rear of the borrowed pickup truck to the back of the yard. "We don't want it to wobble, now do we?" As he struggled by me with creosote and a post-hole digger, he turned to me with a smile and suggested that "we" help instead of talk. "Why me?" I asked.

"Because you are the only one around here who weighs over thirty-two pounds, can carry something heavier than a rag doll, can speak in sentences, and isn't in love with Captain Kangaroo. And it was your idea." He was right . . . it was my idea. It would be big-hearted of me to help, and I decided to do it without argument. I didn't decide, however, to turn myself into his bonded servant.

"Go get the hammer . . . Stick those nails where I can reach them . . . Get David out of my tool box . . . I'd like a drink of water . . Hold that post still . . . Grab that picket . . . Get your hand out of the way . . . The baby is crying . . . Don't slop the paint . . . Don't paint the grass, paint the fence." Something was really wrong. I was doing all the work and he was doing all the talking. That isn't the way things normally go at our house. I didn't like it. I had turned a very fine husband into a tyrant over a silly fence. And I wasn't finished.

It took me about three weeks to realize that we had made another big mistake. The entire fence had been built in the wrong direction.

"That's impossible," Lee said. "You can't build a fence in the wrong direction. Not when you have a small rectangular lot with only one back yard."

"Well, this one is all wrong," I explained, "because you put the fence too far behind the house and you didn't include the back door."

In order for anyone to get from fence to house and from house to fence they had to cross over a wide-open and unrestricted space. My waking hours were spent shuffling little children and a large dog in and out of that fence. My back ached and my hips hurt from the effort.

"I wanna go out," interrupted my scraping gum off the woodwork. "I wanna come in!" kept me from lingering in the bathroom for any length of time. Augie scratched at the door and the children scratched at my heart.

30

"Please," I begged Lee, after dreaming I was impaled on a picket fence while tap-dancing toddlers and big furry dogs joined hands and circled about me singing "Ding-Dong the Witch is Dead," "why can't we just fix the fence so it includes the back door? Then the children can come and go as they please with a sense of freedom and I won't develop migraine headaches at bedtime." He thought the whole thing sounded promising. My headaches were beginning to bother him more than they did me. He agreed to reconstruct the fence one more time if I promised to stay in the house and bake cookies and not come out until he was done.

The first day we had the fence-that-was-connected-to-the-house-and-included-the-back-door went fine. It was a novelty and the children were very polite. "Are you still in there, Mom?" Susan wondered, peering through the screen and into the kitchen.

"Yes, I'm still here."

"Good," she would say as she ran back to the jungle gym.

"Can you hear me singing?" Karen asked as she knocked quietly at the door. "I'm singing and swinging at the same time. I just wanted to let you know I'm having fun."

"I'm glad," I said, and I really was.

"Mom, I think there's a panther in the garbage. Can you come and look?" John had . . . and still has . . . a tremendous imagination. I told him he was safe inside the fence and that it was only the cat from two blocks away. I explained that if it had been a panther Augie would have chased it away. This was not true and Augie and I both knew it, but I didn't want to scare John.

David sat and ate sand all day and was happy. They could play freely, almost unsupervised and without much adult interference. How did I know that it would soon create a whole new set of problems?

How did I know they would go in and out of the house so often? How did I know they would bring 3000 tons of sand inside with them to scatter in the toy box, the beds, and the carpet? How did I know they would drag in enough bugs to qualify us for a full-time forest ranger? How did I know they would smuggle smelly, crushed baby bird shells, homeless kittens, and grubby playmates into our house? How did I know? I didn't, of course. And they not only brought in, they took out. My most expensive bedspread became an Indian tent without my knowledge or consent. The only matching set of dishes we owned played tea party with toadies. My eyebrow pencil wrote funny words on the side of the house.

Almost overnight Karen learned to jimmy the hook on the gate. She passed this secret down from sister to brother to sister much like grandmother passed the old family yeast starter. Getting through the gate and getting mom's goat became a family tradition. Even the dog mastered it.

"We have defeated our purpose," I told Lee. "I can't even make a telephone call. The minute someone sees me on the telephone, every one of them runs out of the gate and leaves the yard to see how far they can get before I hang up."

"Good Lord," Lee said, "they could get to Minnesota. This could be serious." So, he bought a heavy padlock and a tiny key. "There," he said. "We will lock them in. It's not cruel," he added when he saw the look on my face, "we're only being practical." And he handed me the key. I promptly lost it. The lock rusted and the gate was closed forever to children and public alike, and because the fence and locked gate stood, blocking traffic, no one could enter our back door unless I lifted them over the fence or they climbed over themselves.

They could have used the front door, but Augie took it upon himself to become a guard dog. He stood patiently by the front door and waited for the Avon lady to ring the doorbell. She was a perfectly nice lady who often was the only adult I talked to for weeks, except for my husband and Auntie-dear. I looked forward to our semimonthly visits. I didn't buy much from her because at that time David was eating lipstick and John used my powder to make bullets and Susan could use up gallons of fingernail polish in the strangest ways. The poor lady took one look at the fuzzy horror growling in our doorway and was never seen again.

And we didn't get a water bill all summer because I refused to pick the meter man up and pitch him over the fence and he refused to climb it.

"And furthermore," he said, baring his teeth and holding his head at a funny angle as he tried to look down my blouse, "there's no way I am coming through the front door, not with that fool dog in there." He told me his boss could call the governor for all he cared, and left.

I was glad to see him go and glad that I never did see him again, but Lee turned red in the face when he had to pay for a whole year's water consumption at one time. They finally hired a high school boy to read the water meter. He came on Saturday and could vault into our yard like a kangaroo. He didn't have any problems with that locked gate or the fence. Nor did the children. They could scale it in seconds. In fact, David's college reputation as a dorm escape artist was based on skills developed in his own back yard.

Auntie-dear came to spend a few days and peered out the back window at the children playing inside the fence and said something about "Zoo . . . this is like living in a Zoo!" But what can you expect from someone who wouldn't touch anything in the bathroom without spraying it with Lysol first?

4

Please Don't
Drink the Tornado Water

When spring came I sat in our house and wondered if we were all going to be blown away by central Nebraska's notorious wind and end up in a Kansas back yard. I was no Dorothy wanting to whirl up to the Land of Oz with Augie tucked under my arm. In the first place, he was as frightened of storms as I was, and in the second, he was too big for me to carry comfortably.

As a single person I didn't bother with the climate. I just wore a sweater when it was breezy, a coat when it was cold, and as little as possible when it was summer . . . causing Auntie-dear to comment on my morals. I measured the weather by the temperature of my body, not by levels of terror.

When I became a mother I began to worry. Thunderstorm or tornado forecasts brought out a yellow streak in me that reached from the tip of my head to the soles of my feet. Had I been alone and accountable only for my own safety I could have managed. In fact, I could've moved away. Perhaps to the Fiji Islands where nothing happens but coconuts . . . but I had a responsibility—several of them, and a good portion were under the age of five.

The house we lived in when the children were young had the necessary bedrooms, living room, kitchen, bath, and utility room, but it lacked one crucial item. There was no basement. There wasn't even a hole. And I wanted a basement. Especially when the air danced with electricity and trees bent horizontal outside the picture window and the hail beat the hell out of the roof . . . oh, how I wanted a basement! All I had was a bathtub, and you cannot get nine people and a dog in one bathtub.

Surveying our immediate neighborhood, I spent at least three months each year hunting for a friendly, nearby basement. Spring daffodils dozed in the sun; birds romped in the treetops; grass grew green underfoot. It was a beautiful time of the year. Ignoring the seasonal rebirth I mapped appropriate steps to save my life and the lives of our children in the face of a storm. I had a planned routine to put into action the minute a storm warning was announced. Lee pooh-poohed the entire campaign. "Why are you going to so much trouble?" he asked. "If a storm is going to get you, it's going to get you." He has a straightforward philosophical hold on anything remarkable or unusual. He ignores it.

"Well," I said firmly, "if a storm gets *me* . . . it's going to have a fight on its hands. Besides, I don't believe in fate. I believe in preventative measures." He looked at me funny. At last count he was buying cereal for seven children. It was obvious he felt "preventative" was not in my vocabulary. Disregarding his attitude, I assigned each child a duty he was expected to carry out without argument or complaint. I was very firm and insisted we rehearse on nice days. It was Mommy's Civil Defense Plan, and woe to the child who followed in Dad's footsteps and appeared brave in the face of a weather alert. I was in charge and I was scared. I had only to hear the words "storm warning" whispered by the media during the day when Lee wasn't home and I grew weak with fear.

The children knew just what to do. One was responsible for clean diapers, one for full baby bottles, one for cookies, one for coloring books, one for the transistor radio and candles, and one for my cigarettes. I was responsible for the baby. No one ever forgot the diapers, bottles, cookies, coloring books, radio, candles, or cigarettes. Once in a while I had to go back for the baby.

Neighbors never worried when the air grew muggy and the clouds thickened. They went about their business, safe in the assurance they had their own neighborhood built-in alarm system. They needed no sirens or warning whistles. They might miss a siren, but they could never miss the sight of a half-crazed woman with a baby in her arms, trucking down the street followed by an army of small children carrying cookies, coloring books, and cigarettes. Not once were we turned down when I pounded on a neighbor's door. They didn't say, "Goody-goody, I'm glad you're here," but they didn't slam the door in our faces. They opened up, stood aside, and let us into their basements and their hearts. Occasionally, one or two would point out that the sun was still shining and wonder if my panic was a bit premature.

Lee didn't get upset when he came home in the late afternoon to an empty house. He knew we had gone into the ground somewhere. He patiently searched for us from house to house, stopping to chat now and then with a neighbor. Somehow, the minute he appeared I knew it was safe to go home. His being there made up for us not having a basement of our own.

But even Lee didn't help if it was pitch black outside and the wind and the hail and the fury of the storm were upon us and it was too late and too dark and too dumb to hunt for a basement. No one could help me then. Well, Someone could . . . and don't think I didn't ask Him!

"What can I do?" I cried as the lightning flashed and the thunder cracked and the poor trees in our front yard, shivering from whiplash, laid their top branches on the ground in pain. "Where can we go?"

"Nowhere," Lee said calmly. "There is no place to go."

"I can't stand this," I screamed, throwing myself under the bed with a pillow over my head. The dust balls made me sneeze but it beat being tossed in the air. Lee didn't go to sleep, either. He had to stay up because he didn't feel comfortable snuggling down under the covers while I huddled under the bed. He napped in the big chair until the crisis passed and I crawled out for air.

But there came a time when he reminded me what I was doing to the children. "You've got to get ahold of yourself," he said. "You can't continue like this. You are going to give the children a complex, me a bad back, and you are going to strangle yourself on an innerspring. Do something constructive when you are frightened."

I took his advice. I folded clothes, I washed dishes, I opened and closed drapes, I dusted the dog, cried over the children's baby books and pictures, licked trading stamps, read through the check stubs, and generally tried to keep myself busy and calm. I did not fool anyone. And with this sort of upbringing, naturally the children developed complexes. They also developed a healthy respect for the weather. John, now too grown-up to cry, turns a pale gray, Karen nibbles her fingernails down to the elbow, and Mary very quietly takes a pillow, a blanket, cookies, and a good book and sits underneath the pool table until the storm has passed. Mary has outgrown coloring books, but I often wish she was still outlining cute bunny rabbits that have clothes on instead of reading lurid books, but she keeps herself occupied during storms so I suppose I shouldn't split hairs over trifles.

The most inventive child of all was Amy. She had her own "fail-safe" method of dealing with storms. In her preschool mind it was simple, scientific, and very, very secure. She bottled tap water, called it "tornado water" and presented it to me with confidence and a flourish. "Here, Mommy," she said, "put this on the television and when the bad old tornado comes just throw it all over and it will go away."

The "tornado water" sat on our television set for a long, long time. I didn't have any real faith in it. I didn't truly believe that it would ward off bad storms, but it didn't take up much space and I simply pretended not to notice when friends' eyes wandered over to the plain, quart jar with the colorless liquid that decorated our living room.

It was a placid year, weather-wise, and I even mentioned to Lee that maybe we should consider patenting the "tornado water" that sat on our television. "Could be she has something there," I said. "It certainly is cheap, and it does work." He didn't think so. Not even when I pointed out our lack of severe weather did he think so. He said the weatherman would laugh at me if I ever told him—or anybody—about it. But he didn't take it off the television set either.

We didn't have to sprinkle the bottle as days went by and it grew a bit stale and cloudy and some of it evaporated, and Amy gave a little to her grandfather, who lived alone. Spring came and went and we were into an early summer. I hadn't been under the bed in months and everyone talked about the unusual mildness of our weather. Lee looked at me severely and I kept my mouth shut about our family potion. Amy, interested in the new kittens in the neighborhood, forgot her quart jar of water and I grew complacent and moved it from the television set and placed it in the cupboard with the canned goods. I was not quite fearless enough to throw it away . . . I just tucked it in among the jars of beans, pickled beets, and tomato juice.

And then it came! Roaring into the middle of the night! Wind, hail, rain, lightning, thunder . . . the whole enchilada. My composure and the electricity went at the same time. I was horror-stricken. Even Lee looked dismayed when the windows wobbled in and out and the air popped and crackled with danger. Unstrung, I divided my time between cowering under our bed and dashing around licking stamps. It was so dark! I had positioned the children in different corners of the house and covered them with sleeping bags and pillows. I ignored the cries of "I'm smothering!" "Susan is sitting on my stomach!" and "I can't smell anything but David's feet!" and continued my dashing. I bumped into something solid. It was Lee. He asked for stamps to lick.

If Lee was frightened, I knew we were in real trouble. I remembered the "tornado water." Galloping to the cupboard I grabbed the jar, unscrewed the lid, and started frantically flinging the contents around the rooms—up on the walls, on the ceiling, around the furniture, in the corners, under the table. I gave it a good one. Lee muttered "Crazy-lady," but did nothing to stop me.

Eventually the storm moved on. The rain diminished to a trickle, the trees stood straight again, the hail melted, and the lights came back on. We had survived.

"My God!" Lee screamed, clutching my arm. "What have you done?" I looked around to see just what I had done. The house resembled an axe-murderer's paradise. Red splats were splotched everywhere. Living room, kitchen, bedrooms, and bath were redecorated in great, grabbing, bright scarlet polka dots. The children in their pajamas and Augie in his fur stood soaked and very surprised. I had antidemoned everyone with tomato juice. Our house had survived the storm, we were all intact;

it was just ugly. After I washed the children, crawled into bed, and curved cozily next to Lee, I wondered, out loud, if we shouldn't consider a patent after all.

He said he didn't think so . . . and kissed me good night.

5

Hanging Out
the Family Uglies

I often wondered during those preschool days if something crucial had been left out of my makeup and that this lack made motherhood particularly hard for me. Certainly I had lacked a deep interest in infants and children when I was a child. I hardly knew where they came from, and no one had bothered to tell me. Oh, I had heard rumors when I was about ten, but set those aside and concentrated on perfecting my batting stance. First things first, I thought, and confined my concern to trying to peep when my sister changed my nephew's diapers. I didn't even baby-sit. I left that to my friends, and I got a job on weekends, when I was old enough, in our local movie theater ushering and popping corn. Not a very good reference for having babies of my own, but I don't remember Lee asking for a resume on our honeymoon. And on days when I was standing in the kitchen laboring over some unknown quantity in a recipe my mother-in-law had passed on as an easy family favorite, I listened to sounds coming from the boys' bedroom and wondered what had happened to that little girl who was going to be the first female second baseman in the national league. Where had she gone? Where was she headed? To the laundry room, of course. And to the doctor's office and to fetch drinks of water and to rescue toads from the toy box and frogs from the refrigerator, to monitor fist fights and kiss bruises . . . to play tooth fairy and Santa Claus and, after all the children were in bed asleep, to play the centerfold in *Playboy* magazine. I was better at tooth fairy than centerfold.

I took a four-year-old boy aside and told him that he shouldn't call his sister a big B.O. and he asked "Why?" and I didn't have an answer. Anyway, not a good one. He didn't know what B.O. stood for and I didn't have time to explain it to him. Besides, I felt B.O. wasn't so bad . . . he could have called her worse, and did, when they both grew older. I felt inadequate, and continued to feel more inadequate when I listened to other women explain how they hopped happily out of bed every morning, very early, and had everything whipped into shape by noon. I could not quite get over the fact that there were days when I didn't even get the bed made by bedtime.

I knew I was an unfit housekeeper when my automatic dryer died and I wished I could, too. Lee thought it was a blessing in disguise. He said that in this day and age people were far too dependent on machines, and he bought me a clothesline. Not only would a clothesline save electricity and money, he said, but our clothes would smell better, the exercise would do me good, and I'd feel alive and more like getting my work done. "Wanta bet?" I felt like saying, but instead I said, "Thank you, there is nothing I wanted more than a clothesline. Never mind that I don't own pearls, mink, diamonds, or an automatic dryer. A clothesline is much, much better." He was pleased that I liked it.

I had nothing against hanging out clothes. It is a perfectly nice thing to do if you like freezing your knuckles and nose on cold days and getting sunburned and stung by wasps on hot ones. I realized that a good dose of fresh air would be very beneficial in getting the Augie-Doggie smell out of the boys' sheets. But solving one problem led to a multitude of others.

"What problems?" Lee asked. "How can you make a problem out of hanging up clothes? All you have to have is strong fingers, some cheap clothespins, and a basket. The rest is elementary." I told him we needed new clothes. I had no intention of hanging out the clothing we had. The neighbors had seen those clothes dozens of times and were sure to be tired of them by now.

"I don't think the neighbors will even care," he said.

"They will look! I know they will," I cried, and Karen

looked alarmed and asked if I was going to hang her underwear out there for Sam-across-the-street to see. They were entering kindergarten together in the fall, and she didn't want to walk to school with someone who knew everything there was to know.

John and David giggled, knowing they were safe and that I would definitely not consider putting any of the litter that gathered in the bottom of their dresser drawers out for the public to eye. Susan volunteered to look under her bed and gather up as many things as she could so we wouldn't look poor.

My neighbors who owned clotheslines made it a game to see who could get their clothes hung up first. They started very early in the morning. "They must wash all night," I told Lee. "I'd rather watch television."

"But just think," he said, "they get to see the sun come up, hear the birds sing, and have the satisfaction of knowing they are starting the day off with zest and organization. Wouldn't you like that?"

"Not necessarily," I said. I had big problems getting the clothes to look right. Other clotheslines were full of straight little soldiers, categorized by color and graded as to size. Brown towels hung by orange ones in the fall, lime and yellow clung together in the spring, a red sweater dangled seductively next to a white shirt, and stockings were paired and perfectly lined up as to ownership and shoe size. No sock stood alone. And the clothesline didn't sag and nothing touched the ground and nothing . . . not one thing . . . had holes in it.

"What do they do with all their scurvy stuff?" I wondered out loud. A friend told me she didn't wash hers. She threw it all away. "I wouldn't have anything left," I said. "All I have to do is hang it out and a perfectly good dish towel or brand new training pants spring gigantic holes and turn gray." My clothesline looked like a foundling home. I tried hiding the uglies in the middle and putting the big things like sheets on the outside, but that didn't work either. For one thing, sheets hated me. They twisted and turned and scrunched up into wrinkles, and every time I tried to shake them they dipped down to the ground and got dirty on the ends. By the time I

42

finished hanging them up they needed to be taken down and washed all over again. If I lopped them over in the middle, and pinned them up in bunches, they didn't dry. I let the clothes hang when it rained, hoping they would mildew. I rushed out a load when I saw the wind begin to stir, thinking surely they would be whipped to shreds and then, only then, would I prove to Lee that this wasn't a practical solution. I enameled the clothespins in bright paints, put magnets on their bottoms, and gave them away as gifts.

"What am I supposed to do with these things, Mom," John asked, opening his birthday present and finding thirty-two rainbow-colored clothespins packed neatly in a cracker box. "Why, son, you put messages on them and stick them around for people to see and enjoy. You'll have loads of fun with these."

"Oh," he said. He had wanted a basketball.

I tried to destroy the clothesline. I didn't do it maliciously or in any way that would point a definite finger in my direction. I used subtle measures. I told the children they could have a circus. They could use the clothesline as a tight wire or a trapeze, or they could take scissors and cut it up into little pieces and pretend it was snakes. They said their dad would kill them if they did anything like that.

I tried shaming Lee into buying me something velvety and lacy. I told him the neighbors were having weekend company and I wanted to impress them by hanging out something with class. He told me not to be foolish and bought me a charm bracelet with the children's profiles and birth dates on it instead.

I hung out the same old cotton and polyester week after week, and then one day when I was least expecting it a delivery truck backed up to the door and I became the mother of a beautiful automatic dryer. I used the clothesline to dry rugs and blankets, and then just rugs, and gradually nothing at all. The whole thing rotted and tumbled down from neglect, and after a few months I told Lee I missed hanging out clothes.

"After all your complaining, you miss it?" He looked puzzled. "I'll never figure you out."

"Of course I miss it," I said. "It's human nature to miss something you don't have anymore—even if it gives you trouble."

And that is exactly how I felt when the children went to school.

SECTION II

WHEN THE TEACHER TAKES OVER

Kindergarten Through Sixth Grade Stage

6

Too Much Education
Can Be a Dreadful Thing

Karen started school and began to doubt that she had
the smartest mother on the block. Until then I had her
fooled. I was the captain of the team and everyone knew
the rules of the game. When I said that Little Children
turned into screech owls if they stayed up past eight
o'clock, they buried their heads under the covers. I told
them it was possible that a tiny boogie man lurked in
my jewelry box and that scissors were definitely dipped in
poison. A full cookie jar guaranteed that they would follow me anywhere.

No one cared if hand-me-down corduroy pants hit
mid-calf or if their flannel shirts were safety-pinned instead of buttoned or that I made paste from flour and
water instead of buying it at the store. They approved
of peanut butter sandwiches as a luncheon staple and
Jello as a suitable dessert. And they thought I was a great
mother. Of course, they knew no other.

On her first day of school we bought Karen a little
pencil box, a tablet, a book bag, a green shag rug with
her name printed in big black letters on the rubber non-
skid back, and Auntie-dear sent money for a proper desk.
She had brand new shoes and her hair in pigtails with
ribbons on the ends, and I made sure she had a fresh
hankie and a good breakfast under her belt. It was a thrill
to watch her go down the sidewalk, stop to wave one
more time, then continue with confidence toward the
school. Susan, John, David, and Mary lined up each
morning to tell her good-bye and waited for her return

47

to fill them in on what was happening. She did not fail them. She came home each afternoon and exploded every motherhood myth that I had ever used. She had a new leader . . . someone who was not only teaching her to read and write but pounding all the silly nonsense that Mother had put there right out of her head. The Teacher became the experienced one, the possessor of great ability . . . the law. I faded into the kitchen sink, wondering why The Teacher couldn't have said, just once, "Well, maybe," instead of explaining in detail that it was scientifically impossible for a small child to turn into an owl no matter what time it was.

"The Teacher says there is no such thing as a boogie man," Karen proudly told her captive audience of sisters and brothers, "and this means that nothing will bite you or scratch you if you peek in Mommy's jewelry box."

"Don't count on it," I shouted from the kitchen sink. No one paid any attention. Their eyes and ears were fastened on their oldest sister. "And scissors are not poison, The Teacher says." Susan nearly fainted. "And flour and water is messy and anyway, The Teacher says good mommies make biscuits out of those things instead of paste and we should have all the buttons on all of our clothes all of the time because safety pins can be dangerous to little children." She paused triumphantly. I was sweating. "And The Teacher says we should all bathe alone!" A gasp went through the children. They were astonished. For years—as many as they could remember—they had happily jumped into the bathtub, sharing hot water and Ivory soap with anyone who happened to be around. They hadn't insisted on privacy. They hadn't even worried if the door was open or shut and now, all of a sudden, The Teacher says, "Don't do it." Too much education can be a dreadful thing.

The day it was announced in the classroom that babies absolutely did not come from the Montgomery Ward catalogue like Karen Lueth's mommy said was a black one indeed. For years, I had threatened to return one or two of them and get my money back just like the advertisement said I could. It had been a good leverage in times of need. The news traveled through our house like wildfire. Little knots of children gathered, speculating where they might have come from now that good old Montgomery Ward had been ruled out. "A fairy princess brought me, I know," Karen said.

"I think maybe they found me on the fifty-yard line," announced John. He wanted to be a professional line-backer.

"I was Roy Roger's kid," David said.

"I lived with Winnie-the-Pooh once," Mary nodded sadly. "And some day I'll go back there."

"I was an angel in heaven," Susan said dreamily. Everyone gave her a funny look. They could swallow fairy princesses, perhaps, and linebackers, cowboys, and a cartoon character . . . but an angel! Susan didn't fit the mold! Not at that age, anyway—that came later, when she grew up and gave us our first grandson.

"I wonder where we really did come from?" someone suddenly interrupted the conversation. "Let's ask Dad," John said. "He's smart."

"Ask your mother," smart Dad said.

"Don't ask me," I told them. "Ask The Teacher. Let her explain. She's been doing a marvelous job up until now."

7

Augie-Doggie, the Star

Karen seemed to learn to read overnight. It was one of the biggest thrills of my entire life. When *Dick, Jane,* and *Sally* came alive on her lips, I got goose pimples.

"Isn't it marvelous to hear her read?" I told Lee. He looked a little weary, but agreed it was quite an accomplishment. Now that I look back on it, I think he might have preferred hearing something from *Sports Illustrated,* but was too kind to say so.

I could hardly wait for her to come home from school each day. I would meet her at the door with tingling spine. "What did Spot do today?" I asked, hanging in spellbound suspense for her answer.

"He jumped!" she said dramatically.

I caught my breath. Let the rest of the world travel, spend money, or watch soap operas to pep up their days . . . I had Spot!

She read each day's lesson to the family after dinner. It became a ritual. Dad, Mother, brothers, and sisters gathered around. "Go, Puff, go!" she read. I clapped my hands in excitement.

"Run, Dick, run!"

I urged her not to stop.

"See, Sally, run and go!"

John said it was a boring story and wanted to know when the cowboys came in.

"He's too young to appreciate good literature," I apologized.

Along about the fifth or sixth child the newness wore off. Spot had jumped just about as much as I could stand to see any dog jump. I still listened, but I have to admit

50

my heart wasn't always in it. I, too, turned to other things for excitement, but once in a while I caught myself wondering what the three of them had been up to. Dick, Jane, and Sally eventually faded into the background like the children's baby pictures.

But in the beginning I was anxious to become involved in school activities. Pet Week was no exception. Because Karen cried and said that Ernie's mother had brought a bull snake to school the day before and even let it wrap itself around her and couldn't I please bring Augie-Doggie for a little while so he could do a few tricks and everyone could see him and besides she had promised The Teacher and could I be there at one o'clock between lunch and recess so she would miss math? Of course, I said "Yes." And in my opinion that makes me much more of a mother than my friend who said she wouldn't take their dog to school on a bet and anyone who did must not be too bright and she was going shopping and if I had any sense at all I'd forget the Pet Week business and come along. I didn't. I wish I had.

You see, Augie is not your common, ordinary, bright-eyed bushy-tailed little house pet. He is a BIG dog, covered with wiry, lush, rampant hair . . . a dog who had an Afro long before they became fashionable. He did not prance on tippy-toes, he whomped. He seldom saw where he was going or what he was doing. His hair covered his eyes just enough so that he felt his way around by using his nose and one paw. He liked it that way. The one time we trimmed the hair around his eyes he hid in the basement for days afterward. Therefore, we just let him grope.

I was not anxious to show Augie off. Nor could I find him. One hour before we were due in the classroom he disappeared. I told the little children to look up and down the block, without crossing the street, to see if they could find him. I called Lee at his office. He said to stand outside and yell, "We're having a barbecue in the back yard!"

Amy found him sitting in a neighbor's yard smelling like a skunk and looking very pleased with himself. I quickly ran hot water in the bathtub, threw Augie in, and prayed Lee would never find out. One thing he couldn't tolerate was a dog in his bathtub. A friend who was a veterinarian once told Lee that a dog's fleas caused impotency. Although they had both been sampling martinis,

Lee still didn't want to take any chances. I didn't have time to worry if fleas might sever my husband's sexual pleasures forever. I had to get Augie in shape so he wouldn't embarrass Karen. And he looked dandy when I took him out of the tub. I looked rather warped, but I had no time to groom myself, I had spent it grooming a very ungrateful dog. "Oh well," I thought, "no one will pay any attention to me anyway. They will all look at Augie and he will be so perfect, so cute, so well-mannered and well-trained they won't even notice me."

I had never met the Teacher and I hated the thought of bursting in on her resembling a crow, but math class was due to start and time was running out. I couldn't find a leash, so I grabbed Lee's belt as we went out the door.

Throughout the entire trip to the school I tried boosting Augie's confidence. "Just be yourself," I told him. "Remember how you sit up and beg? Why, you do it better than any dog I know. Don't worry about anything. I'll be with you all the time." He licked the window and seemed relaxed. I suppose Augie and I set Pet Week back about a hundred and fifty years. Poor little children, still unborn, could be faced with a public school education that has eliminated Pet Week. Perhaps even Show and Tell. I don't know exactly when things started going wrong. I was willing, the teacher was willing, the classroom was willing. It was Augie that messed things up.

He behaved perfectly until we reached the school grounds. I had no reason to be suspicious until I opened the car door and he shot about the school yard, lifting his leg and grinning. Yes, grinning. And then he rolled on the ground. The condition of the ground he rolled on was not favorable for rolling. I think another dog had been there before him . . . and I think Augie picked that spot on purpose. I doubted anyone would be fooled into thinking the light brown tinge on his shoulder was natural. He smelled awful. But I was the adult—I was the human being—I was in control. I slipped the belt around his collar, whispered in his ear that there would be no more funny stuff, and led him sedately up the sidewalk. As we neared the classroom, I shifted my shoulders, donned the appropriate parental smile, and prepared a grand entrance.

Augie saw the children. He could not wait to get his

paws on them and he lunged into the classroom. The belt immediately shortened and I was jerked like a marionette, but I held on. I couldn't let loose, as a matter of fact. Any ideas I had about meeting The Teacher with elegance and poise were gone. One arm was being jerked out of its socket as Augie thrust ahead, tightening the belt even further, and as a consequence choking himself and emitting a terrifying sound. Little girls dropped into their seats and brave little boys turned pale. Karen tried to leave the room. The teacher gripped her desk, her welcoming smile froze on her gray face. "Ye gods," she shouted, forgetting that she was The Teacher, as Augie continued to make his way around the classroom. Suddenly he stopped and threw up. One snicker sounded in the right-hand corner of the left row. One boy had seen the humor in the situation. The rest followed. They all began to laugh. Augie sat down, inclined his head, and thumped his tail. He was a star! He put out a paw to the child nearest him.

"He stinks!" the child said, gagging. Everyone laughed— louder. This was Augie's cue. He was on stage again. He began rushing around the room—and throwing up. My control had deteriorated to zero. My only thought was to get out of that room immediately without speaking to The Teacher. But she spoiled that plan. She wanted to see tricks. After all, we had promised tricks, and she wasn't going to let us off easily. Personally, I thought we had displayed plenty.

Until this moment, Karen had not acknowledged that this was her dog, or her mother. She had worked on her math and cleared away enough homework to last for several weeks. With a sigh, she put down her pencil, came to the corner of the room where I stood shivering, took the belt from my partially paralyzed hand, and went to the front of the room. Augie was all hers!

"Sit up, Augie," Karen commanded. Augie tickled her hand with his tongue. "Roll over, Augie," she said. He stood transfixed, a silly smile on his face. "Play dead," she hissed in his ear, and with winged feet he shot away, waltzing by the teacher, charging into a row of seats, and galloping about the room. The children were having the time of their lives. They urged him on by shouting, clapping, and stamping their feet. "Go, Augie, go," they chanted as he swooped about the room. I tried to follow and grab the belt. "Go, Mrs. Lueth, go," the children cheered. We went around the room three complete turns. Augie was exhausted. I was exhausted. We were both wheezing. But we were going home. Pet Week was over for Augie-Doggie and his surrogate mother.

"Good-bye, Augie," I heard The Teacher call out as we sneaked out the door. "Do come back and visit us again soon."

8

Beyond
the Call of Duty

"Do you realize," I told Lee one morning in early October, "that we have more children in school than anyone else in the neighborhood? Do you realize the teachers presented me with a 'Beyond The Call of Duty' award when I attended five classroom open houses in one afternoon? Do you realize that I am the only mother who is never asked to be a Room Mother because they feel sorry for me?"

"Are you sure it's that—or could it be the cookies you sent that time for Mary's birthday and made everyone sick?" It could have been. I hadn't really given it any thought. Mold grew profusely on the woodwork as I entered elementary school with each child and learned to color-coordinate their stockings so they wouldn't stand out, to attack the clothes hamper with a vengeance so they would be super-clean, and to prepare nourishing meals so they would look well-fed. I knew I had to be twice as good as the lady down the street with the two well-spaced children so people wouldn't say, "Why did she have so many kids if she can't take the proper care of them?" Others could send their children to school with Kook-Aid and dust streaks running down their elbows and no breakfast in their stomachs, but I couldn't. At least, I wouldn't.

Cooking was particularly difficult for me. It still is. But I was determined that when our children stood before the classroom and answered "What did you have for breakfast this morning?" none of them was going to say,

"Raisins and radishes," and have the teacher write a nasty note to the school nurse suggesting she drop in and visit with that Lueth lady about nutrition. I knew a good breakfast meant the start of a good day . . . for everyone but me. I whipped out of bed at 5:30 in the morning. I don't cook quick, either. I brought out the cookbook, poured a cup of strong coffee, dug the sleep from my eyes, and made out the breakfast menu. Pork sausage links, scrambled eggs, juice, milk, toast, and strawberry jam. My God, I was proud. It took eighteen sausages, two dozen eggs, twelve fluid ounces of frozen orange juice, three quarts of milk, twenty pieces of toast, and one broken jar of jam. The jar slipped out of my dozing fingers as I removed it from the refrigerator. At that particular moment I didn't think life was very fair to mothers.

Lee was sleeping, the children were sleeping, and the birds in the trees were sleeping while I was sitting in a cold kitchen picking slivers of jam-covered glass from my wrists. Raisins and radishes were suddenly appealing.

I put the sausages in the skillet, added a small amount of water, and watched them swell to great proportions. Huge blisters popped out on the sides of each link. I ran to the cookbook to see what was happening. "Do not prick," the cookbook warned. The sausages were expanding rapidly; they were coming out of the pan and were in great danger of falling into the flames below.

"I've got to prick," I said to the wall, "or they'll explode!" Cautiously I jabbed a fork tine into the biggest sausage of them all. It looked alive. "Phhhttt," it went, and grease spattered on the stove, on the walls, and on my forehead. The wounded sausage immediately shriveled to the size of my little finger and turned coal black. Others grew to take its place. It was prick or perish. Wrapping a towel around my face and arms I attacked the sausages on their ground. Prick, prick, prick, I went. Phhhttt, phhhttt, phhhttt . . . they went. Now I had a pan of tiny burnt sausages . . . not a decent link in the lot. Never mind, I thought, I'll just cover them with scrambled eggs.

By now, Lee and the children were coming into the kitchen in various stages of undress and disorganization, having been awakened by all the "phhhttt, phhhttt, phhhttts" and my unfortunate choice of words describing the heritage of the sausages. "Tie my shoes, Mommy," Amy pleaded. "I can't," I told her, "my hands are all wrapped up. I don't have fingers. Ask your dad."

"He's taking Claudia to the bathroom and yelling at the boys," she said, sitting beneath my feet to examine her toes.

"Tell Susan to tie your shoes."

"She won't. I already asked. She's hunting her homework. She thinks she left it outside."

I cracked the eggs by bringing them together between my towel-wrapped hands and creating friction. True, a few shells showed here and there, but I'd probably get those picked out in time and if I didn't, I was sure I had read that eggshells contained calcium.

"Why do you have a towel on your face?" Lee asked as he bent over to kiss me good morning. "You look funny. So do the eggs." Those eggs weren't scrambling. They were poaching, and they smelled like iron. It must have been the calcium. But never mind, I thought, no one will notice.

Someone noticed. "I won't eat guts," John said. "I want cereal!"

"I want cereal, too," another said, and another and another.

"Hell, we'll all have cereal," I shouted, and dumped shriveled sausages and soggy eggs in the sink. The toast had burned black and the orange juice was warm. Mary cried because I had killed the little chickens that rested in the eggs and then cold-bloodedly tossed them away. She was sifting through the mess, tears pouring from her eyes, looking for a feather to prove that her mother was a killer. "Leave the garbage alone, wash your hands, get your shoes tied, find your homework, quit throwing raisins, eat your radishes, and for goodness sakes, will someone please say the prayer and thank God for all this good food." Lee said he didn't think the Good Lord had stuck around long enough to hear a prayer.

It wasn't that I didn't have great dietary hopes when Karen was born. Preparing her formula had been equal to a scientific research program at M.I.T. I weighed everything carefully and measured it for nutritional balance in a sterile, disinfected corner of our kitchen. It took me two or three hours to prepare formula. The first time she ate out of the dog's dish I called the doctor. He laughed. I called my mother. She laughed. I called Lee. He came right home from work. He was like that and still is, I'm happy to say. He too believed that germs were bad for babies. "But look," Lee said, "she is eating chunky stuff with dog gravy on it better than she does your strained squash. She isn't spitting it out."

"Well, she's not going to eat dog food," I gagged. Augie looked relieved.

It was not easy finding a suitable substitute. I tried chopped zucchini. She started racing Augie to his dish when she heard the sack rattle. Eggplant made us all look longingly toward the Gravy Train. And then I created my own monster. I did it myself. I discovered cold cereal. It became my Mother's Crutch. As long as I knew I had a full box of cereal in the cupboard I knew we were going to eat. As cribs multiplied in our bedrooms, cereal boxes took root in the kitchen pantry. We had no room for flour, sugar, or salt. Canned peas grew cobwebs behind toasted flakes of corn. Cereal became a staple and all-purpose substitute. Lee worried that our Thanksgiving dinner some year would consist of sweet potatoes and Grapenuts. I told him he was being silly. Once a year we would eat real food . . . I didn't have to give into the children's whims three hundred and sixty-five days a year. Fortunately, the children did not notice that schoolmates spoke highly of roast beef and mashed potatoes, and brought soft chocolate cookies as birthday treats. I sent Rice Krispies soaked in marshmallows that tasted like sticky stones. Lee grew used to checking his clothes every morning for clinging puffs of rice before he went to work, and I thought nothing of spending thirty minutes each day picking sugar-coated globs off the bottoms of seven pairs of fuzzy-footed pajamas. It was our life style, and we accepted it. The oven died of neglect, the crock pot cracked from inactivity, and the electric can opener gradually deteriorated. All we needed were spoons and milk. Claudia grew up thinking the entire world looked like a Cheerio. If she cried, I gave her a handful to munch on.

If she smiled, she got a bunch. When I needed to sweep the floor, wash windows, or clean out a cupboard I simply dumped a pile on her high chair tray. Learning to grasp little circles definitely improved her eye-to-finger control. She is, to this day, our only ambidextrous child. Lee complained a little about having to buy so much cereal, but I noticed that he made sure there was plenty in the house when he had to baby-sit. I suppose a father needs a crutch as much as anybody.

9

Saved by a Germ

I had married with great expectations. I had grand thoughts of living three months in Las Vegas, three months in Paris, three in the Hawaiian Islands, and the remaining three dropping in on Academy Award presentations, dancing at inaugural balls, and fighting off lewd advances from Robert Redford, John Davidson, and Johnny Carson behind Lee's back. I was going to have a whirling social life.

I had no idea that the maximum high would be centered around planning and attending a Blue and Gold Cub Scout banquet once a year with the Cubmaster—my husband. Lee had accepted this position when John was a brand new Cub Scout because no one else in the neighborhood would do it. I was his social secretary. It did not pay well. I was also a Den Mother. This did not pay well either. I did have one slight advantage over the other Den Mothers, however . . . I was sleeping with the Cubmaster.

Cub Scout pack meetings were designed to bring all dens in one area together once a month to receive awards and to compare projects, bruises, and Den Mothers. Lee presided over these monthly meetings. He was assisted by a Pack Committee that met over coffee and doughnuts to talk football, bank loans, and lawns. Occasionally they nodded in his direction and said, "You handle it." Our first pack meeting did not go well. Ten dens with an average of eight boys per den added up to an awful lot of noise and confusion. And for some reason, when the Pack Committee turned to Lee and said, "You handle it," he thought eighty little boys would be fascinated with a forty-five minute slide showing of *The Import-Export Grain Business In Great Britain*. They weren't. They stampeded. One nearly choked to death in the punch bowl, another ripped off twenty-three dozen chocolate chip cookies and all the Arrow Awards under Wolf, and the other seventy-eight made the Golden Gloves look like a sissy happening. Lee felt he had failed. He immediately offered to resign. The Pack Committee wouldn't let him. They clapped him on the back, pumped his hand, and said, "You can handle it. We are behind you one hundred percent. Be sure and call on us if you need us," and went home, put their feet up, had a gin and tonic, and relaxed. Lee went home, had an Alka Seltzer, harbored muscle spasms, and planned the next month's meeting.

John told his dad not to worry about it. "The kids love our pack meetings, Dad," he said. "They think you're a neat Cubmaster. You don't blow your whistle and yell like all the others." Our pack meetings became the most popular monthly sport around town. None of the parents wanted to come, none of the Den Mothers wanted to come, and quite truthfully, the Cubmaster didn't want to come. But John was right . . . the Cub Scouts loved it. Every kid in town wanted to be a Cub Scout. Even the Girl Scouts.

Weekly den meetings were held at our house every Monday afternoon after school. I spent the morning unplugging fourteen bottles of Elmer's glue and stapling the furniture to the floor. Augie pranced in anticipation two hours before the boys arrived, and the cat hid behind the freezer. The Assistant Den Mother and I frisked the boys as they entered the house. We removed all sharp pencils, insects, bubble gum, and pornographic literature. The girls stayed as far from the house as possible, because they couldn't stand being with so many nine-year-old boys. When I ran out of things to glue and games to play, I fell back on the Den Mother's dearest way out . . . "The Tour." Some tours lasted longer than others. One lasted exactly three minutes, which was long enough to walk in the front door of a greenhouse and out the back. The minute I said, "Cubs, remember, stay together!" yellow kerchiefs and jeaned legs squirted in a million different directions, romping through the rhododendrons, gallivanting in the glads, and mobbing the marigolds. The owner was backed up against the sprinkling system with a seedy expression on his face and his hand on the automatic sprinkler switch. One squashed snapdragon and I'm positive he would have drowned us all. Apparently, though, the boys didn't mind our meetings, because most of them grew up to be Boy Scouts. The one who screwed up the Kool Aid when it was his turn to add the sugar, got a terrible shock when he unplugged the table lamp, who needed help from a friend to cut paper rabbits for decorations and didn't know how to thread a needle went on to get his Eagle Scout award, and I stood in the audience with everyone else had tears in my eyes and felt maybe our time and effort had paid off, after all.

I carried some guilt, however, and wondered if perhaps I shouldn't be serving something for supper other than popcorn and jelly bread on Mondays. The house appeared to be falling apart from maternal neglect. Lee decided maybe I should have help with the housework. He said if I had someone in to do the heavy cleaning, then I would have more time for simple things like cooking, laundry, sewing, bookkeeping, mending, ironing, and being his A-number-one Den Mother. He said I might even be able to find his lost slipper, sweater, and pipe that had disappeared, lo, those many weeks ago. I hope he never gets an idea like that one again.

Two days before the cleaning woman was scheduled to come in with her mop and broom he asked me why I was washing walls.

"Because they are very dirty," I answered.

"Leave them for the cleaning woman."

"And let her see how dirty we are? Not on your life!"

"Do you mean you are going to clean the house before she comes?" He was stunned.

Of course I was. What red-blooded, American housewife wouldn't? A woman knows that the only way to present a first-time, strange housecleaner with a house to clean is to present it c-l-e-a-n. I rehung pictures, rearranged knick-knacks, painted the kitchen table, washed the curtains, changed the beds, dusted bed springs, and relined the kitchen shelves. I was careful to leave one bread crumb, a half-empty package of macaroni, and a pencil stub beside my sparkling dishes. I wasn't going to get caught napping. I didn't want her thinking I had been messing around in there. I had to leave some natural clutter.

I warned the children to leave one pair of underpants on the floor next to their beds. This caused real speculation and big eyes. They hadn't heard an order like that before. I told them to be sure it was a clean pair without torn elastic.

"But I don't have any without torn elastic!" John complained.

"Borrow David's, and just do it!" I said.

I cleaned Augie's dog dish and changed his place mat. He looked cross when he sniffed and didn't find the good old familiar stale odor. His corner smelled suspiciously of ammonia and scrub water. It ruined his appetite. I didn't allow anyone to bathe for two days so the tub's gleaming perfection shouldn't be spoiled before the cleaning woman came. Giving the bathroom one last delicate swipe, I carefully placed a tiny squirt of toothpaste in the upper left hand corner of the glass and put a colorful piece of lint right on top. "Perfect!" I announced to the dazzling chrome. For emphasis I laid the toothpaste tube, squeezed tightly from the bottom, on the corner of the sink. I left the cap off for reality and, with pure genius, hid it behind the wastebasket. This would give me the opportunity to complain about husbands and children and how they messed things up.

Lee's lost slipper was found in the hall closet beneath the jigsaw puzzles, his sweater in the toy box wrapped around a large teddy bear, and his pipe under the stereo with my real leather coin purse. Moving to the closets, I rearranged the clothes, sizing them to fit like straight Marines, with their shoulders thrown back and their fannies tucked in. I placed one wire hanger on the floor between Lee's hunting boots and a pair of starched, white tennis shoes with brand new unknotted shoe strings. Dramatically I draped a pair of freshly laundered, no-run pantyhose (size X-Small) across the toe of one of the shoes. It looked a little messy but smelled divine.

Using a Q-tip, I bleached the children's baby teeth, saved over the years and tucked into envelopes, and was about to sponge down the cedar tree beside the front door when the telephone rang. "Mrs. Lude?" a hoarse voice said. "I habe an awful code. I can't clean."

Saved by a germ. Hallelujah!

But to waste all of this once-in-a-lifetime cleanliness was more than I could bear. And because few people have a glowing cedar tree growing by their front door I decided to have a party to show it off.

"I will invite every good housekeeper I know," I told Lee.

"Even Auntie-dear?" he said. Especially Auntie-dear I decided.

10

Who Needs Money, Anyway?

"You are to be envied, you know," Auntie-dear said, flipping cracker crumbs off the kitchen table. "You have a handsome husband and all those darling children to keep you company in your old age. You'll never know the word 'alone.'" She almost sounded wistful. "Alone" sounded delicious to me. "Alone" sounded wonderful. "Alone" sounded like trumpets and sparklers and seventy-nine trombones. "Alone" sounded impossible.

Karen was in the sixth grade; Susan, fifth; John, third; David, first; Mary was anticipating kindergarten, and Amy and Claudia were hanging around the house keeping me from becoming bored with things like afternoon naps, reading a good book, or having lunch downtown with friends. The initial scare of hiring a cleaning woman had faded into the past and the house had reverted to its jungle state. Lee felt comfortable about putting his feet up on the couch, and I didn't clean under the bed. I didn't blame Auntie-dear. She was probably right, at that. But while she was having the fun of telling me how to raise the children—I was having the fun of doing it. I often woke up in the morning and felt sorry for myself. I decided I needed a job. An identity. I wanted to be important at coffee breaks, instead of sharing them with a cat who only wanted to lick my cup. People in business would appreciate me for what I was, not for my ability to pack a functional diaper bag or make solid Jello. I could earn my very own money and not have to rely on a child's piggy bank to pay the Avon lady.

What I really had in mind was the presidency of some large corporation. A Joan Crawford-type position. If a person could shuffle swimming lessons, tap dancing lessons, guitar lessons, piano lessons, orthodontist appointments, school play rehearsals, Brownie meetings, Cub Scout meetings, parent-teacher conferences, and birthday parties, surely handling a bunch of employees would be simplicity itself. I didn't tell the family of my intentions. I was going to stun them all with the announcement that I was going to add, oh, about $30,000, at least, to the household budget. I planned to bake an angel food cake for this celebration.

Dressing up in my good old go-to-the-PTA, go-to-a-funeral, go-to-the-dentist brown suit, I left the little girls with a neighbor and went to the first employment agency I could find. As I walked in the agency door, I broke out into a cold sweat and the palms of my hands itched. I was about as poised as a damp cornflake. The receptionist guarding the agency looked suave, extraordinarily intelligent, and seven feet tall. My brown suit wrinkled before her eyes, my pantyhose sagged, and lipstick appeared on my teeth. Thrusting a complicated sheet of paper and a ballpoint pen under my nose, she said in an automatic voice, "You will be given twelve minutes to complete this test. Do not look until I tell you. Now get-ready-set GO!" and she pushed a button on an enormous alarm clock and went back to the book she had been reading when I interrupted her. I could tell she had not classified me as executive material. I was reduced to pudding.

The first question was to list ten things I did well. I listed (1) Answer telephone nicely. (2) Can comb and set Barbie hair. (3) Wield automatic can opener with skill. (4) Measure detergent accurately. (5) Can speak fluent three-year-old. (6) Can maneuver oven controls. (7) Can sweep floors well. (8) Empty vacuum cleaner bags without spilling. (9) Good grocery-cart pusher. (10) Not bad in bed. I scratched that out.

The next page of questions ran from quotes from Shakespeare to geometric diagrams designed to test my ability to think things through. I reached the middle of the third page and decided my I.Q. fluctuated between a minus 20 and a minus 25. I sort of sighed when I came to the mathematics part of the test. I could've handled something like "Farmer Brown has three cows . . ." but they wanted to know items like "At $48 per M what will it cost to cover, with two-inch planking, the floor of a barn measuring 24 × 42 feet?" A teardrop fell. For one thing, I didn't even know what M stood for. Was it Mile? Was it Minute? Was it Mouse? I wrote down, "Hell, who cares?" I scratched that out.

The clock went off. My spine twitched. By now, I had lost two buttons off my suit, my hose rested around my ankles and I had to go to the bathroom. I was led to the typewriter and told that now I could take a typing test. I already knew how to type. Sort of. But I knew my skill would definitely be hampered by that silly clock at my elbow, ticking like a time bomb. "This is a time test," the receptionist yawned. "You will be docked for every error you make." I could have sworn she grinned when she said it. My concentration was shattered and my test came out something like this: "People dis oled hog proc es vu they loke high woges excepr whein haiving youpay thim! 'any were criticll in 1930 whin a no . . . people discloke shigh prices, but they like ghut woges. Escept whm the havinf to pacy them! Many were icruieicx." Phooey! My head ached, my bright red teeth hurt, my palms itched, and shooting pains darted in and out of my toes. I sat there with my back straight, facing that typewriter, and knew that I DID NOT WANT TO GO TO WORK. I wanted to go home.

I really didn't have to worry about getting a job, anyway. The stuck-up receptionist whinnied, "Don't call us, we'll call you," and chucked my test in the wastebasket. I shot out of that office and went back to my familiar, cluttered kitchen. Rubbing my hand gently over the grease smears, I kissed my dirty oven and baked an angel food cake to celebrate. Who needed $30,000 anyway? Eventually, of course, I did go back to work, but the children were older and my reasons were different. I didn't go to work because of a bad attitude. I went to work because inflation and college tuition just happened to arrive at the same time at our house. But that's another story and another chapter. In the meantime, I concentrated on remembering how lucky I was.

Lee always had faith that I would develop a marvelous

capacity for efficiency and organization. He didn't seem to think it was at all unusual to come home in the evening to find me leafing through my recipe file, trying to decide on something original to do with burnt swiss steak. He was as unconcerned about my producing botulism as he was about my producing babies. He never once complained about diapers left to soak in the bathtub or Crayola marks on the coffee table or talcum powder on his good suit or the fact that his wife usually sported fourteen circles under each eye, safety pins instead of jewelry, and a caress that was like touching fingertips with an American buffalo. He accepted all of this, and declared he wouldn't change one single thing about his life. Well, maybe, he said, he wouldn't mind replacing our clunky station wagon with a sports car, it would be nice if we didn't have to buy shoes every time we went shopping, and wouldn't it be pleasant to go a whole month without a trip to the emergency room?

Surely, I thought, people in other houses were more structured than we were. The whole world couldn't live like we did. Oh, I knew kings and queens didn't, and presidents and tycoons, and our doctor, but I was thinking about ordinary, average families. From the first day of school until late spring I didn't drink one cup of hot coffee at my kitchen table. By the time I dressed Claudia and Amy, helped Mary, found David's shoes, iodined John's latest wound, located a clean blouse for Susan, soothed Karen's hurt feelings over a lost necklace, ironed a shirt for Lee, and kissed them all good-bye, any coffee poured was lukewarm and tasted like bitterroot. I grew used to it. In fact, I could hardly tolerate the rich, steaming coffee served in friends' homes and restaurants. To this day I still prefer cold coffee to hot.

Old habits, like old husbands, are hard to throw away.

11

If Holidays Are for Kids, Why Does Mom Work So Hard?

I couldn't wait for holidays. They happened to be my specialty. We celebrated everything except Yom Kippur, and that's because we were Presbyterian. For instance . . . Halloween . . . I was usually glad when it was over! For one thing, I could get rid of that silly jack-o-lantern with the green teeth and the puckered nose. And Lee started speaking to me again. It had been touch and go for a few days. I realized there was nothing in our marriage vows that involved him in trick-or-treating, but I was desperate. I needed his help. So did the children. He had thought it was a grand idea when I suggested Claudia, Amy, and Mary dress up as The Three Little Pigs. He had thought I was using my head when I turned their warm, pink, fuzzy-footed pajamas into piggy suits. He laughed when he saw the cute, curly tails sewn on their tiny bottoms and the little ears attached to their heads.

"They'll be the hit of the neighborhood," he said proudly, patting them on their pudgy, pillow-stuffed tummies. He put a quarter in their sacks, took up the evening paper, sat down in his chair, and prepared to spend a quiet Halloween night in front of the television. The Three Little Pigs began to cry.

"I promised them a wolf," I said quietly.

"That's nice," he replied, taking off his shoes.

"I need a wolf."

"I think there's one in the refrigerator." And he put another log on the fire.

"You're not listening!" I accused.

69

"How can I, with The Three Little Pigs crying? Why are they crying?"

"Because I told them you would be their wolf."

"I will not be a wolf."

"Well, someone has to be. I promised. That's the only way I could get them to dress up like pigs. They wanted to be potato chips."

"You be the wolf," Lee suggested.

"Who ever heard of a woman-wolf? Every wolf I know has been a man. Besides, I have to stay here and hand out treats."

"I'll hand out treats," John volunteered.

"You'll eat them."

"Let him be the wolf," Lee said.

"He's too young to be a wolf," I was quite positive about that.

The Three Little Pigs began to cry louder and in unison. Their pink ears were starting to droop and their tails were straightening. Lee weakened enough to say, "I don't know what a wolf does."

"Just walk around and look ferocious."

"And scare every kid in the neighborhood. I'm not the type."

"You don't have to attack," I told him. "Just huff and puff." I ran to get his costume. I wasn't going to let him back out now, as I had spent all afternoon getting it ready. Of course, he didn't know this. I think he suspected, though. Ordinarily his corduroy trousers didn't have a furry black tail protruding from strategic seams nor did his hunting cap have long-tipped ears sticking out from the top.

"I won't wear ears and tail," he said firmly. The Three Little Pigs began to cry.

"I don't think people will know you are a wolf unless you dress the part," I said, arranging his tail to its best advantage. I drew large circles around his eyes, painted his nose red, gave him whiskers, and carefully placed plastic fangs in his mouth. "There now," I admired. "You make a handsome wolf. The nicest one I've ever seen."

"Jubst wiaghtl I gebt homble," he mumbled. He seemed to have difficulty talking with fangs in his mouth. I hung a sign around his neck that read "Please Do Not Feed," and handed him a burlap bag. I told him he could tuck one of the little pigs in the bag, put another under his arm, and take the third by the hand. In that way he could keep them all under control and still remain in character.

"Jubst wiaghtl I gebt homble."

I stood in our door as they went down the sidewalk to join the Halloween fun. The Big Bad Wolf looked quite cross and one little pig squealed because she was being grasped pretty hard by a paw. I thought they looked darling. And it was easy to follow their progress through the neighborhood. Porch lights flickered on, and shrieks of delight split the evening air as I heard, "Good God, Arlene, will you come here and look at this!" I knew they must be having a terrific time.

I hated to leave the doorway to answer the telephone when it rang. It was a good friend about six houses down the street. She told me she had answered the doorbell and found this fully grown rather snarly human-looking wolf with three crying little pigs standing outside. The wolf had asked for a beer and told her to call his wife and give her a message. She said she thought it was Lee. I told her I thought she was probably right and asked for the message. She said she wasn't sure but she thought he said something like, "Just wait until I get home."

She wondered if I had a message back. I told her to tell him to hurry home. I told her to tell him that he might be surprised what a good wolf could get by with, if he played his cards right. After all, kids weren't the only ones that could trick or treat!

Thanksgiving . . .

"Hello, Turkey. I'm hungry."

"Hello, Pilgrim. Here, eat me."

Don't you suppose that's how it all got started? In a way, I wish the Pilgrims had started us all off with something a little simpler. We could just as well have celebrated Thanksgiving with hamburgers, french fries, and cole slaw or something equally delicatessenlike. A turkey takes so long to fix, especially if you forget to take it out of the freezer. A frozen turkey is very difficult to stuff and truss. For the first ten years of my life as the designated family cook, I failed to take the turkey out of the freezer in time for it to thaw for proper preparation. Little tentacles of ice dripped from the dressing as I wrestled, half-asleep, preparing the turkey for the oven. You try getting up at 3 a.m. and plunging your hand into a frozen carcass—I think you'll understand my feelings. Naturally, with such pithy preparations, we didn't eat our holiday dinner until late evening, and by that time Claudia and Amy were falling asleep and parts of the turkey were still raw. The mashed potatoes weren't bad and the celery sticks were unusually crisp, but no one wanted to eat potatoes and celery at 10:30 p.m. Karen complained that she hated going to school every year and writing in her Thanksgiving essay that all we had to eat was potatoes, celery, and marshmallows. I told her to lie and draw huge pictures.

Lee grew tired of this charade, and decided to solve the problem in his own masculine way. No more frozen turkeys and romantic late-night Thanskgiving dinners, thank you, not for him. He brought home a real, live turkey . . . tied up in a gunny sack. A red beard peeked through the holes of the bag, beady eyes jutted through the holes, spurred feet flapped in the breeze as Lee carried our Thanksgiving dinner into the garage.

"Oh boy," clapped the children, following right behind him. "A real live turkey. Fresh. Not frozen. Just like our Pilgrim Fathers." A pox on the Pilgrims, I thought. "Thanksgiving is three days away," I said. "What do you propose to do with this turkey until then?" Lee looked at me as if I had no common sense at all. "Let him live here in the garage," he said.

"In that gunny sack? How cruel! What will the neighbors think?"

Lee told me the turkey would be fine. That he could move around and that if I looked in on him once in a while and fed him and watered him we would have a prize bird for our dinner table. I didn't realize that I would develop a fondness for that turkey.

"Poor old fellow," I said, placing cracked corn and water before him each morning. He gobbled back pitifully and tried to bite my hand. I didn't take it personally. I understood why he might react that way. I wouldn't be too gracious, either, if someone was fattening me up to kill me.

When execution day dawned, I didn't want to have any part of the kill. But Lee told me I was the only one big enough and strong enough to hang on to the body properly. "I just can't!" I screamed.

"Yes, you can," he laughed callously. I had been living with a cold-blooded axe murderer for years and didn't know it. "Just pick it up, hold it over the stump, and close your eyes."

That grand old bird looked up at me with pleading eyes. His feathers drooped. He looked almost skinny. I thought fondly of the frozen turkeys of the past and wished for them to return in all their icy splendor.

"It will just take a second," Lee said, running his thumb along the razorlike sharpness of the axe edge. I alternated between fainting from the fear he might whack off my hand to wondering if I could snatch Old Tom to my breast, hold him close, and plead for a pardon for both of us. The turkey dressed out to twenty-two and a half pounds, and he looked so vulnerable with all his feathers gone, sitting there bronzed and naked on the platter. I almost wished for a while that I had let him eat at least one of my fingers. Poor thing, he had so little in life. I couldn't eat any turkey. It was like feasting on an uncle. I ate a lot of potatoes and celery and marshmallows that day. But I'll tell you one thing. I always remember to take the Thanksgiving turkey out of the freezer.

Christmas . . . Christmas would have been my favorite holiday if we hadn't taken the children shopping. It was like unleashing Snow White and the Seven Dwarfs. Guess who was Snow White! We went one time per season when the children were small. That was it. We gathered up mittens, coats, pocketbooks, lists, and children and went to the largest discount department store in the area. It had everything from toilet water to Tonka toys. Before we left, I stood in the middle of our untidy cottage and gave instructions. "Try to remember that Santa has quite a burden. He is responsible for millions of little boys and girls. Let us not stand in front of the expensive toys and finger the boxes and look wistful and whimper at strangers when they pass by. And cut out the fighting in public. We don't scuffle in housewares."

And so Snow White and her seven children set out. Doc is the leader. He marches into the store, grabs a shopping cart with great confidence, and runs down the first little old lady he can find. With $1.98 in his jeans for Christmas presents, he knows just how he is going to spend it, and it takes him fifteen minutes to do his shopping. He now has three or four hours to make a nuisance of himself while the rest of us try to pick out our presents.

Sleepy begins to yawn the minute we leave the car in the parking lot. Now, Sleepy has had a twelve-hour nap in his own little bed, but the sights and smells of a shopping center render him sluggish. Trying to rest as he walks along, hanging onto my cart, he stumbles, head down, obviously snoring. People are looking at him . . . and me. I stick him in my cart and he immediately falls into a deep sleep and enjoys the entire shopping trip covered with gift-wrapped packages.

Sneezy is allergic, and cannot enter the sections that contain live Christmas trees, perfumes, and scented soaps, the food department, or the aisle where they sell wool shirts. He is confined to hardware, and is bored out of his mind. He is forced to buy the same old thing every Christmas. We all graciously accept screwdrivers, tacks, silver wrenches, and bolts from Sneezy when the presents are passed around. I never lose Sneezy . . . I just listen for his wheezing, and carry plenty of handkerchiefs.

As for Bashful . . . Bashful is a bombshell. He has been talking of nothing but Santa for weeks. But when he comes face to face with this jolly old man he becomes frozen with fear. He stands in front of Santa's throne with his little head buried in a display of marked-down merchandise, while brothers and sisters gaily throw themselves on Santa's lap and pour out their hearts. Santa reaches out his hand to Bashful in a friendly gesture, and Bashful screams as if he has been attacked. Bashful cries all the way home because he didn't get to talk to Santa. It was all Snow White's fault!

Happy makes the most of the whole day. Nothing bothers Happy. He has lost his mittens, one snowboot, and his Christmas money. He doesn't care. He's found his holiday paradise. He sits among the toys and methodically breaks the cellophane on twenty-three boxes. He is still smiling when Snow White picks him up in the lost and found department.

Dopey draws a crowd. Dopey turns somersaults and cartwheels in the area that displays the sign "You can touch—you can hold—but if it is broken—consider it sold." I have an enviable collection of chipped china. I am probably the only mother in the world that has a complete forty-piece service of elegant dishes that are in four hundred platinum-trimmed pieces. That's all I received for Christmas that year, by the way. Dopey is quite a shopper, bless his little heart.

Grumpy is probably the worst one, though. And Grumpies come in many sizes. They don't necessarily have to be small. Sometimes old Grumpy is bigger than I am, and called DAD. Little Grumpies cry and kick and get spanked behind the drapery department, but big Grumpies stand around like they have sacks on their feet and count their money. They don't get spanked, but they get lots of dirty looks from Snow White.

When the shopping trip is over, the cottage is all cleaned up and the Christmas tree lights sparkle and dance and it is warm and cozy and all the little dwarfs are in bed . . . Prince Charming is really my favorite, hands down.

Easter . . . Every year the do-gooders of America staged a bunny hunt in a local park. And we were always there. All except Lee, that is. He used the weak excuse that someone in the family had to work to buy the alfalfa pellets for the rabbit our children were sure to find. Hide that grand prize egg wrapped in aluminum foil, and John was sure to be the first one to discover it. He had an uncanny nose for chocolate eggs . . . especially ones with a live rabbit attached. Now, he could not find his clean socks, his homework, his toothbrush, his pajama bottoms, his lunch money, his way to the garbage can, or his underwear, but he could always find that damn prize egg. Days before the scheduled hunt, he would explore the area where the hunt was to be held, mapping out a categorical and specific plan of action. "It will be somewhere in here," he said to David, Mary, Amy, and Claudia. Karen and Susan were too "old" to hunt eggs . . . they were hunting boys, by now. John pointed out a squat bush sketched in on a roughly drawn diagram of the neighborhood park. "They always put it in a place like this. The Park Lady who hides it is fat. She can't stretch and she can't bend over." The four younger children were fascinated with his obvious grown-up, big-brother knowledge. "Here's what we have to do," he continued. He told David that he had to be the one to run interference. David puffed up like an All-American. "It will be up to you to grab any kid who looks as if he is following me."

"The Park Lady will throw me out," David complained. "She always does. Why can't I find the egg and you get called a bully for a change?" Ignoring him, John turned to the three little girls. "You cry," he ordered. "Just stand there and cry. The ladies will all give you candy and the other kids will watch. This will give me time to make my move." Claudia, Amy, and Mary began to practice. Great tears streamed down their faces. Could I listen to this sobbing trio for six days? I could not!

"I don't know what to do," I told Lee. "They are going to find that rabbit egg again this year, mark my words. We're going to have that rabbit in our house." He grinned. "And I will get stuck with that poor little bunny. The children will get bored with it after three hours and then it's mine. Someone always lets it hop around in the house and Augie stalks it and terrifies it—and you know what happens to scared rabbits."

"Don't take them to the hunt," Lee suggested. "It's as simple as that. There's no rule that says you have to take them." I was shocked. I couldn't ruin their pysches forever. What mother would deprive her children of an Easter Egg Hunt? I wouldn't have it on my conscience.

Naturally, the Saturday before Easter dawned bright and beautiful and clear. The hunt was on. The children were excited and had outfitted the annual cage with soft rags and crisp carrots. A polished tuna can was filled with fresh water. It was a hutch with real class.

We were among the first to arrive at the park. Children spilled in from every direction. Whispered strategy and large paper sacks were passed out. The Fat Park Lady looked smug. She knew where the aluminum-foiled egg was hidden, and she had blatantly lied to her own child.

She wasn't going to be foster mother to a rabbit. I didn't have that assurance. David was doing deep-knee bends and flexing his muscles. Claudia, Amy, and Mary were whimpering quietly. John was poised for action. He rubbed his fingertips together much like Sam the Safecracker. He was primed to go. But just as he prepared to spring out, a stout arm plucked him from the starting line. "How old are you?" a strong, solid voice asked. "Ten," John answered. "Too old, too bad"—and John was swept out of the starting line. The Fat Park Lady had made the rules and that was that. "It's the breaks of the game," I told him. I couldn't help but be a little pleased. I promised to buy him some candy eggs now that I felt our chances of having a rabbit in the family had dropped by ninety-five per cent.

A commotion in the middle of the park attracted my attention. I heard screaming and scuffling. It was the Fat Park Lady and her son. He was wailing and she was wrestling a large, foil-wrapped golden egg from between his clutched fists. "You can't have it," the boy yelled. "It's mine!"

"And you can't have that rotten rabbit!" she yelled back. Mothers on the sideline joined in. "He won it fair and square." "Let the kid alone." "It's his rabbit, for God's sake, let him keep it!" John stood quietly by my side, looking quite happy for someone who had just lost out on the Golden Egg. "I wonder how that boy knew where the Rabbit Egg was?" I said. "He certainly found it in a hurry."

"I'll never tell," John smiled. "But I bet the Fat Park Lady lets me play next year."

12

For Goodness Sake
Don't Tell Mommy

Whatever I thought about my life in general was immaterial as I steeled myself to face one important event. The Last Day of School. The children and their teachers celebrated, and I endured. Claudia, Amy, and Mary were thrilled to have their older brothers and sisters home again to bring variety to their lives, Augie was tickled pink, and I vowed to set some rules and regulations and bring order to chaos. I was not going to spend another summer ranting and raving to a bunch of kids who drank nothing stronger than Kool-Aid. "Look," I pointed out, "Mr. Green Jeans makes his bed . . . so does Mr. Bunny Rabbit. I don't know why you can't follow their example. Captain Kangaroo says 'Make your bed' and a rabbit makes his bed. When rabbits are more cooperative than human children someone has failed." Everyone looked at me.

"Maybe if you came dancing and singing and smiling into the kitchen like the Captain, Mom, we'd do better," Susan said with a very sweet look on her face. She was right. Amy said she'd make her bed and make me happy again, but she couldn't reach it. No one else volunteered. Well, I thought, there are some good points to a summer vacation. Not a bunch—but some. I wouldn't have to attend any more elementary school band programs for three whole months. That alone should have done a lot to make me cheerful. And no more parent-teacher conferences, no more heavy research projects with Karen on the sixth-grade viewpoint of the sex life of a snail, no early hunt-the-homework crisis, no more diagnostic decisions on just how sore a throat was or how much a head hurt or if the cramps were real or imaginary or caused by eating too many tacos. No more hauling of reluctant bodies from between the sheets so they could make it to school before the tardy bell. I certainly didn't have to worry about anyone sleeping during the summer months. All seven immediately developed an aversion to sleep. Beds became a place to stash stuffed animals, good spoons from the kitchen, potato chip sacks, used bubble gum, toy trucks, water guns, and sand. Lots of sand. Blessed be the bed that held a child's body for more than eight hours during summer vacation.

"Why do I have to go to bed?" David asked. "The sun is still up and there is no school tomorrow." It was 11 p.m. and he was barely seven years old. And he had gone through a very busy day. So had I. We had all been up since 6:30 a.m. . . . since the first slamming of a door. Knowing Lee was still snoring by my side, the sun was snoring in the clouds, and it was very early in the morning, I wanted to know who was going out that door.

"Who is leaving and where are you going?" I shouted.

"It is David and I am going out!"

"Where out?" I really wanted to know. "I don't want you wandering around empty streets. You could get mugged."

"Everyone else is up," he explained, coming into the bedroom. "Come and look. The streets aren't empty." And he was right. The neighborhood was bustling with activity. Little red tricycles with tiny drivers in training pants bombed up and down sidewalks, and young mothers in baby-dolls hauled naked toddlers out of sand boxes. Augie and his friends gathered beneath the streetlight, which was still on, by the way, and the daddies, bless 'em, on their way to work were tucking good tools in brief cases for safekeeping. And it was only the first of June.

"Don't get so upset," Lee said as he packed his tools in the car and prepared to run away to his quiet office and uninterrupted bathroom privileges. "Establish a routine and stick with it. I'll draw up a list of recommendations and if you get everyone to follow them your summer will be a snap. Remember, YOU are the mother. They are the children."

Well, I already knew that. It was the children he had to convince.

After stashing his tools in their proper place he came into the house that evening and proudly presented me with a list. "Guaranteed results," he grinned. "If you'll just follow these suggestions . . .

1. No one is to leave the house for any reason before 9 a.m.

2. Children shall remain in rooms tidying up, meditating, or reading about snails, while allowing Mother to sit down and have at least one cup of coffee.

3. Once outside, stay out! Necessary body functions are to be attended to BEFORE leaving the house.

4. No door slamming. EVER!

5. Absolutely no fighting. Not with brothers and sisters, not with neighbor kids, and definitely not with neighbor mothers.

6. Learn and practice a summer craft. Weaving, knitting, sketching in charcoal, and/or clay pots recommended.

7. Develop a business. Thrift is the key word. Have an adventure with a lemonade stand.

8. Everyone will be bathed, fed, pajamad and ready to discuss the day's events and hop into bed when Dad arrives home in the evening.

I wondered who was supposed to teach crafts, make lemonade, and still have the strength to feed and pajama everyone as I glanced over the last three rules. I knew who *he* had in mind.

Ordinarily, I tossed out rules, thinking they were meant to be bent, twisted, or snapped off at the roots, and this is a bit how I felt about Lee's summertime regulations. But he usually had good ideas, and the least I could do was be a good sport. What could I lose? After one day of following those rules I knew it was going to be the longest summer vacation in history. Here's how it went.

1. *Keep children in house until 9 a.m.* Oh, I kept them in all right. But I let Augie out. Who wants a dog-in-great-pain hanging around the house? The children pressed their little faces to the picture window and watched as their friends and playmates exploded from their house to our house. After answering the front door thirty-two times, the back door sixty-seven times, and hauling fourteen preschoolers out of our garage, I gave in and sent all seven outside. "Don't tell Daddy," I said, "and we'll just forget that rule."

2. *Rest quietly in rooms until Mom finishes a cup of coffee.* Well, I burned my tongue on exactly one-fourth cup before I realized that was a dumb rule. No child rests quietly in a room unless he is very ill or up to something. Ours were not sick. I discovered Claudia carefully coloring her room with black crayon, John tying his underwear together for an escape through the bedroom window, Karen poring over one of the paperbacks I had stashed in my sewing basket because I knew sex and thread would cause no problems. She was quiet . . . but flushed. Susan had painted her toenails, as well as Amy's and Mary's, to the joint with bright fuschia polish and was advancing on David, who cowered in the corner, brandishing a yardstick, ready to poke her eyes out if she got one drop of it on him. "Don't tell Daddy," I said, "and we'll just forget that rule."

3. *Once out . . . stay out!* Now that wasn't practical at all. Have you ever tried to tell a pleading and sobbing child, standing at the door with crossed legs, that he cannot come inside the house for any reason? His only alternative was the neighbor's tulip bed and I couldn't have that. Not in broad daylight, anyway. "Don't tell Daddy," I said, "and we'll just forget that rule."

4. *Don't slam the door.* Everyone knows that door-slamming is instinctive to children. Everyone but Lee, that is. I tried to explain that the ability to shut a door softly is left out of the bone formation of anyone under sixteen. After that they learn quickly. After midnight teenagers have a knack of shutting a door as quietly as cotton on cotton. Lee pooh-poohed my explanation and

told me to try getting the children to be quiet. So I gave lessons on closing a door without shoving the screen in. I took each child aside and demonstrated how to open the door and slip it into proper position before entering the house, and then carried through the entire process of gracefully turning around, putting one hand on the handle and one on the frame, and silently settling the door into position with elegance and without sound. After John strained his right wrist with this unnatural movement, I said, "Don't tell Daddy, and we'll forget that rule."

5. *No fighting.* Boy, I agreed with that one. I don't like fighting and I don't like getting involved and I certainly don't like standing out in the middle of the road and having some other mother tell me my child is a big bully as all the other mothers nod in agreement. I hated having my child take the blame for something that was obviously not his fault. I destroyed warm relationships with every woman that lived within a radius of four blocks and finally told the kids they would have to settle squabbles in their own way and unless blood was drawn I wanted no part of it. "We know," they said, "don't tell Daddy, and we will just forget that rule." They were as happy about it as I was. They loved a good fight.

6. *Practice a summer craft.* I felt summer crafts were fine for city recreational directors and Scout camps, but I don't believe any ordinary mother should voluntarily tangle herself up with a bunch of yarn and children that have ten thumbs. Good Lord, I couldn't teach John to knit. Tears streamed down his face as he huddled behind the couch with the knitting needles clutched under his T-shirt so no one could see him doing woman's work. "Don't tell Daddy," I said as I patted his head, "and we will just forget that rule."

7. *Develop a business adventure.* Fine in theory, but not very practical. It cost me my good crystal pitcher, two sets of glasses, $24, and my best friend. First my children were accused of selling lemonade that gave three neighborhood children diarrhea just as they were leaving for a three-week trip to Canada. Then my best friend had the audacity to say that after helping my kids out, her husband had developed stomach cramps and missed two days'

work. I told her not to blame the lemonade. I told her she might have an autopsy performed on her pot roast. After all, I had eaten at her house once or twice myself. This is when she said she would probably never speak to me again and I said, "Don't tell Daddy, but we will just forget that rule."

8. *Have the children bathed, fed, and pajamad before Daddy comes home from work.* I didn't even try. I substituted. I sent the children to their grandmother's, bathed in perfumed bubble bath, and put on my fanciest nightie. I was prepared to display what there was to display and discuss what there was to discuss and somehow he never did get around to asking about those silly rules. Somehow I managed to get through a lot of summers without them, and besides, rules became inconsequential, obsolete, and very foolish . . . we were entering the junior high stage and it was Katie Bar the Door. Our lives were going to change.

SECTION III

MISCHIEF
IN THEIR POCKETS

Junior High Stage

13

I Really Do Love To Move

Each of our children entered junior high school with a different thought in mind. Karen, for instance, decided to marry at thirteen. She discovered b-o-y-s. The telephone burst forth with adolescent, cracking voices—"MayI speaktoKarenplease,thankyou"—very polite and somewhat nervous if I answered the phone. If Sue answered, she giggled and wouldn't let Karen talk. If John or David answered, they visited about football, basketball, and fishing, and wouldn't let Karen talk. If Mary answered she wouldn't let anyone talk. Amy and Claudia weren't allowed to answer the telephone, and if by some unusual circumstances Lee answered, the boys on the other end immediately became tongue-tied and terrified. So would you, if a profound and thundering voice bellowed WHO IS THIS? and promptly hung up. Lee felt every boy over twelve was a potential rapist, and no daughter of his was going "out" with boys until she was at least thirty-two years old. I gently nudged his memory and told him to look back on his own adolescence. Perhaps that is why he thought every boy over the age of twelve was a potential rapist.

It was exciting to have a daughter in junior high. "Now," I thought, "I will have someone to talk to. She is growing up and will confide in me. We will sit on her bed and exchange secrets and she will share her day and we will become best friends." But we stayed mother and daughter . . . it was better that way. I really didn't want a thirteen-year-old best friend. I don't need to tell you how she felt.

Auntie-dear warned me about the awful things that went on when a child went into junior high. "She will become casual about her dress," she said, peering into her tea cup to see if I had become casual about my dishwashing. "And she will become mouthy and she will be exposed to loud, boisterous boys and she will learn about sex!" And she finished off her tea with one triumphant slurp. I thought of the snail and told Auntie-dear that she already knew about sex, having learned about it in the sixth grade.

Naturally, Karen asked me not to put down how many brothers and sisters she had on the school registration form. "They don't need to know everything," she said. "Besides, the home room teacher always reads it and then says, 'So, you're the oldest of seven children. Tsk, tsk.' She always seems surprised that I have enough money for lunch." I told her some day she would be happy and proud that she had so many brothers and sisters. She said, "Why?" and is still asking the same question some fifteen years later. I didn't have an answer for her then, and I don't now. It's funny, though—she's the first one to send birthday cards and remember anniversaries and make thought-out, individual Christmas gifts for everyone and plan family get-togethers and say, "No one has to bring a thing, I'll do it all." She must have found something out, wouldn't you say? I wish she'd tell me.

Some went into junior high with a smile on their faces and mischief in their pockets. I became involved in trying to cram growing bodies into a shrinking house. Everything in the house became smaller. We were so crowded I couldn't find a place to keep the broom. Sometimes I propped it up beside the television, sometimes I kept it in the play pen with Claudia, sometimes I leaned it against the refrigerator, and sometimes I placed it in the middle of the living room floor so Lee could fall over it and ask the inevitable question, "Why don't you put the broom where it belongs?" I had only to open the door to the small, compact broom closet where it belonged to show him why I didn't keep it there. The broom closet was full of stereo records, last year's straw hats, a hunting jacket, ten pounds of potatoes, two or three used bleach bottles, six cardboard boxes, a tackle box, and four cartons of old Christmas cards. There was certainly no room for a broom.

There was no doubt we needed a larger house and no doubt that Lee and I would disagree on what we needed. He wanted a modest, compact, freshly built cheap house. I wanted a rambling, old-fashioned, stately, gingerbread, curlicued house in the $80,000 or $90,000 range. We ended up with a modest, compact, freshly built cheap house that eventually cost $80,000 or $90,000 after the contractors added superfluous stuff to the original blueprints like plumbing, a kitchen sink, electrical wiring, windows, closets, and a stairway. The frothy things that one shouldn't be without for comfortable living. Building our own house didn't happen overnight. First we looked. We looked a lot. For weeks we haunted real estate offices and for weeks every realtor in town broke out in a cold sweat when his telephone rang, thinking it might be me, wanting to tour a listing. I loved looking at houses. Lee hated it. I liked having a legitimate reason to peek into someone else's closets and kitchen. I saw some terrific medicine cabinets. You'd be surprised what people keep there. It stimulated me for months. Lee said it made him uncomfortable, looking in a perfect stranger's bedroom and pawing through the corners. One house was gorgeous. It was complete with china closets, chandeliers, golden woodwork, stainless-steel kitchen, and all-white carpeting. I visualized shooting the children full of tranquilizers every morning with their Rice Krispies in order to be in a house like that. I hated to give it up, but reality is reality. I fell in love with that one, but the look on Lee's face and the feeling in my housekeeping heart made me know I had to let it go.

A huge white house, three galloping stories high, with a rounded front porch and a grand, polished winding staircase off a foyer the size of two of our present bedrooms and a plain wooden stairway off the kitchen caught my eye. I supposed the stairway in the back was for the hired help. I could see myself, sitting in the spacious bay window, impressing Auntie-dear by inviting the governor's wife to tea, while Brunhilda prepared succulence in the kitchen, Agnes scrubbed the floor, Phoebe amused the children in the nursery, and Jake pruned the hedge and cultivated the roses. Sort of an "Upstairs, Downstairs" kind of life. Lee ruined this daydream by pointing out the condemned sign next door, the six bedrooms that all had crevices between the woodwork, the furnace that looked ready to explode, and the fact that I was destined to be Brunhilda, Agnes, Phoebe, and probably Jake. I sat in a charming breakfast nook and cried my eyes out before I gave that one up.

Lee got tired of peering into strange bedrooms and I became discouraged. After all, if you've seen one medicine cabinet you've seen them all, so we bought a lot, hired a building firm, and built our own house and our own medicine cabinets and then faced the fact that we were eventually going to have to pack up all the kids, furniture, clothes, what-nots, animals, left-overs and m-o-v-e.

I really do love to move. The thrill of seeing the people up and down the street react when two pretty crummy-looking adults, seven pretty crummy-looking children, and one very crummy-looking dog spew from the front and back end of a U-haul truck never wears off. I didn't tell them that we were nice people and that I did own dress-up clothes. I just let them sit there and wonder. I heard later that rumors had flown all around the block as we were moving in. I heard that I was twenty years older than my husband (Lee loved that one), that we had twelve children and I was expecting another in two weeks, that Augie-Doggie was a retired army dog who had served in World War II, Korea, and Viet Nam and was trained to kill at the flick of a wrist; our cats had mange and that the husband had a pretty good job but the pregnant lady just sat home and didn't do much but write stuff that didn't sell. I won't say our new neighbors stampeded and built chain-link fences when we moved in, but I did warn the children not to leave the yard for the next three weeks except to go to school.

I should have told Lee the same thing, for he picked the third day after we moved into our new home to take a business trip to Dallas. He swore it was unavoidable. The fact that he had a ticket on the fifty-yard line to watch the

Dallas Cowboys tucked in his breast pocket and a smile on his face made me wonder a little about how sad he was because he was going. He promised to bring presents, skipped up the loading ramp, waved good-bye, and squeezed the hand of a brassy blonde stewardess who helped him with his topcoat. Only his attache case looked lonely and grief-stricken about leaving as he disappeared into the airplane.

I was left in a strange new house with strange new neighbors, furniture in the wrong rooms, and tons of stuff still in boxes. I also had a fear of burglers, mass murderers, and perverts. Lee was more than three hundred miles away, and my only protection consisted of a sociable dog and two little boys, ages eight and ten, who knew so little about the manly art of self-defense that they still called boxing gloves "boxing mittens" and spent more time trying to tie the laces than they did in actual combat. I couldn't help but worry a little. In fact, I worried a lot. I roamed about the house unpacking boxes with one eye looking over my shoulder for an attacker and my spine tensed to fight back if one appeared. Night time was particularly bad. With daylight peeking in the windows I had an even chance of identifying strange objects, but when it was pitch dark outside I was at the mercy of anyone who happened to wander by. Augie was as scared as I was. He stood at the foot of our bed looking at me with big eyes, and I'm sure would have hopped in beside me if I had only given the word.

Lee hadn't been gone two days when I looked out the kitchen window and watched our back yard begin to sink out of sight. It truly was . . . just caving in. A giant concave circle was spreading and spreading and spreading . . . around and around and around. I felt that any moment our entire household would disappear into the ground and Lee would come home, expecting a big welcome from his little family, and he would find nothing but a hole. We would be gone, and more than likely the brassy blonde would get my present. It hadn't rained, so it couldn't be a mud slide, and quicksand is seldom found in the suburbs and I was reluctant to ask the advice of a brand new neighbor. I didn't want to knock on a comparative stranger's door and say, "Good morning, I am your next-door neighbor but not for long, our back yard is disappearing and I will soon be sucked into the soil."

I could only call Lee and get his advice and/or tell him good-bye and ask him not to marry too soon after my memorial service. He was in an important conference when I called. I could hear him panting as he answered the telephone. "What's wrong?" he gasped. "Is someone hurt? Why did you call? Tell me!" He was really worried, bless his heart.

"The back yard is disappearing." I laid it right on the line.

"My God," he screamed. "Who disappeared? How long have they been gone? Have you called the police?"

"Not who!" I shouted. "What! THE BACK YARD. IT IS SINKING AWAY. THE HOUSE WILL BE NEXT!" I yelled as loud as I could so he could understand.

"You don't have to speak so loud," he said primly, his voice sounding like iced tea. Frosty. Really frosty. "You called me out of an important conference to tell me the back yard is sinking?" Personally, I thought that was reason enough.

"It isn't sinking . . ." he continued. "It's settling. That's where the septic tank is buried. The soil is only shifting and it's not dangerous." Well, I didn't know that. After all, septic tanks and their territories weren't my favorite subjects in school. We exchanged a few pleasantries and I asked him about the Dallas Cowboys and one of the children got on the extension and begged him to come home because they were tired of eating gravy bread and Mommy was acting funny and talking to her dress form and letting Augie sleep with her. This seemed to upset him more than the sinking septic tank.

14

Modern-Day Pinocchio

Can you imagine our surprise when children who had been
content to wear just any old thing, as long as it was bigger
than a handkerchief and smaller than a tent, suddenly became clothes-conscious? "No one in junior high wears
peter pan collars, Mother," Karen told me critically when
I insisted she slip a little something underneath the pecu-
liar loose-knit sweater she was wearing. "And I'm not
going to wear a stocking cap or carry a purse or put on
those silly shoes with laces. You want me to look funny.
You want me to be an old maid." I wanted no such thing.
At that particular moment I would have married her off
to the first person who knocked on the door. Suddenly,
according to her standards, everything about her was
wrong. I thought she looked just fine. I thought her pretty
face and her eyes and long brown hair were exactly what
we would have ordered had we had a chance to do so.
"Look at these ugly bangs," she moaned. "They are
crooked and long and bushy and so awful I can't go to
school. Not like this." She had been wearing her hair in
the same style since she was three years old and never
complained.

"Let me trim your bangs," I offered kindly.

"Don't touch me. Dear God, don't touch me!" she
screamed. "Daddy, Daddy, don't let her touch me!" She
threw herself into a stunned Lee's arms as he walked into
the room. I thought for a minute she was having a spell
and I should call the doctor. Here it was 7:30 in the
morning and our oldest child was on the verge of collapse
over a hairdo. I wondered how she would react when she
discovered she didn't have a bust! It could be fatal, I

thought. I decided never to mention it. And in time, of course, this worked itself out to everyone's satisfaction.

She had never worried about clothes before. None of them did . . . until they entered junior high. I often wondered if the principal was Yves St. Laurent. During elementary school they had worn flannel shirts with seersucker shorts, tartan plaid boleros teamed with polka-dotted skirts, velour with cotton, velvet, and blue jeans . . . if it was handy and didn't have a lot of dog hair on it, they wore it to school. I could order stuff on sale from the catalogue and they didn't turn up their noses and flounce around the room and ask if they were adopted. Eventually, of course, they learned to loathe every single thing that hung in their closets unless it had an exclusive label, cost over $25, or belonged to someone else.

"Where did you get that blouse?" I asked Susan one day when she flew into the house, looking happier than she had in months.

"It's Annie's," she answered. "Isn't it the darlingest thing you've ever seen?" She was purely beaming with pride and satisfaction. The blouse looked like a rag. Three buttons hung by threads, the collar curled on the ends from laundry exhaustion, the colors were faded from a scarlet red to a muted mauve, and it was at least two sizes too large. "Her mother got it at the hospital auxiliary thrift shop. It only cost sixty-five cents. I love it!"

"Where's *your* blouse?" I asked. I had paid $2 a square inch for her blouse. Susan had gone into the dressing room and cried because she was the only girl in the eighth grade who did not own a one hundred percent cotton top, trimmed with Irish lace and hand embroidered, to wear with her jeans. So I bought it. I had the feeling Annie now had two and Susan none. I was right.

"Oh, I gave that old thing to Annie," she said. "We traded. HER mother didn't say anything. HER mother smiled and patted us on the back and told us how proud she was that we always wanted to look nice. HER mother baked chocolate chip cookies and let us eat as many as we wanted. HER mother was all dressed up and had on high heels and earrings and she didn't gripe because we traded clothes." Quite frankly, I wanted to strangle HER mother but I didn't. I made Susan go back and get her own blouse and she didn't speak to me for about three hours. Not until I had baked chocolate chip cookies and let her eat as many as she wanted. But I didn't put on high heels and earrings. Enough's enough.

With heated passion the girls locked themselves in the bathroom and dressed for school each morning. Lee paced nervously outside the door waiting his turn. "Hurry up in there," he shouted, pounding on the door, as Karen and Susan took turns looking in the mirror. "I'll be late for work and if I am and I lose my job, there goes your lunch money." It didn't make a dent. I suggested he get up earlier and sneak in while no one was looking—or perhaps build another bathroom. "I am not going to get out of bed at three-thirty in the morning in order to shave," he said. "And we have no place for another bathroom unless you want one outside." There were times when I would've given my right arm for one outside. It could have been built in a tree for all I cared. Just so it was empty when I needed it.

The girls ignored television, the radio, the dog, cats, brothers, sisters, mother, and father and took up hair-combing as a hobby. They combed their hair so often I warned them it was going to fall out by the roots if they didn't stop plowing their scalps with a fine-toothed comb every three minutes. Long, straight hair appeared on the soap, in the sink, on the vanity, in the medicine cabinet, on the begonia plant, wound around the shampoo bottle, twisted in the woodwork, and cuddled quietly on the light fixtures. John gagged every time he brushed his teeth, which was about once every six weeks, and claimed he'd rather have cavities than die of hair balls in his stomach. Lee insisted they were all going to be bald before they were sixteen and more than likely he would eventually end up with five unmarried daughters with no hair and they would have to live with us the rest of their lives and he would never get a chance to shower or shave again as long as he lived.

The boys didn't drop hair because they didn't have any. Their dad saw to that. Once a month, like clockwork, Lee took them to the basement and swiftly sheared their heads to the nubbin. He was into home barbering and kept his instruments as honed and polished as any surgeon's. And he took it so seriously. I really expected, at any time, to be called to his side, made to wear a green gown, mask, and cloth cap while slapping clippers and comb in his palm. The boys didn't seem to mind, and sat up tall and straight on the high stool and patiently let their dad cut every hair on their heads down to a mere patch scattered at random over their skulls. Their ears stood out horizontally from their heads, their eyes looked hollow, and their scalps showed through, shiny and bright, when he finished. They looked terrible, but Lee convinced me it was a practical way to keep them neat and clean. And it didn't have to be combed because there was nothing there. During the winter they ran the danger of chillblains, but they wore heavy fat stocking caps that mashed their ears flat and left ridges on their foreheads.

Then John entered junior high and declared that only marines wore their hair cut so short and only poor people had their hair cut at home. David agreed, and we entered the period when the boys wore their hair as long as the girls and I began to worry that perhaps *they* would never marry and would spend the rest of their lives living with us. Lee was crushed. During their teens, neither boy would spend more than three minutes alone with him in the basement for fear he would forcibly cut their hair. The barbering tools were eventually tucked away behind the barrel with the baby clothes and left to rust. Just the other day, Lee looked at our grandson and wistfully said, "Don't you think he could use a haircut? I bet I still have those old clippers of mine." The baby was immediately snatched up by his mother and taken home before grandpa got any more ideas. She remembered when her brothers looked like skinned onions.

Since we didn't have $65,000 per child to spend on new clothes and haircuts, I was determined to protect with my life that which we did have. That is why I was sometimes found by a puzzled husband chasing a cricket around the living room with a vacuum cleaner hose. Basically, I realized that crickets were harmless, but they were noisy, quite homely, and ate clothes. And the crickets at our house didn't eat the clothes I wanted them to. I offered the children's grubbies and they turned up their noses. I prepared a gourmet meal of patched blue jeans and stringy sweat-

shirts, put them in the corner and included a centerpiece of tube socks, and then called in every direction, "Here, little crickets. Come and get it." Not one cricket appeared. Turning up little feelers at my prepared menu, they chomped their way through my best nightgowns.

"Ungrateful beasts," I muttered, and took Augie aside for a long talk. I sat down on the couch beside him, put my hand gently on his head, and said, "Look, dog, we have never expected you to be a retriever. We have never expected you to be a champion in the field. You have led a sheltered dog's life. Where are your instincts? Where is your doggie pride?" He licked my hand. "I am only asking a simple thing. Get those crickets! Sniff them out! Bark! Bite! Use your paws! Use your tail! Just get them!" Augie was no killer, not even of crickets, and no one else in our house would smash a cricket voluntarily. They had no qualms about snuffing out the lives of spiders, ants, moths, or my African violets, but let a cricket cross their path and it was as if royalty had entered the room.

"Don't kill him," Susan screamed as I approached a dark corner with a rolled up newspaper. "It's bad luck. You are never supposed to kill a cricket in the house. Something awful will happen to all of us if you do. My science teacher said so."

"Something awful is already happening. I will not hav these nasty little buggers parading through the chip ar dip in front of Auntie-dear."

"They're only being friendly," Lee grinned.

"Friendly or not," I said, "they had no business hopp up on her lap and just sitting there rubbing their b legs together. It was obscene."

"Open the door and let the cricket jump out," Lee gested.

"How can that help? If I open the door for the or go out, three thousand more come in. Besides, how d know he even knows where the door is? Crickets can' They don't have eyes. They have antennae. They The children were impressed. They didn't know I things like that.

"Show him the way," Lee said. "Poke him with thing. Guide him. He is just a tiny cricket. He c can't hurt you."

I knew that. I knew that crickets don't bite. I turned to John. "As oldest son, you have responsibilities. Get that cricket!"

"Don't look at me," he said. "I'm not going to kill a cricket. I have all the bad luck I can handle now."

"Do you want them to eat your tennis shoes?" I asked.

"They won't eat my tennis shoes." And he was right. Not even a cricket was that desperate.

"I'll shoot it with Dad's shotgun," offered David eagerly.

"I'll get it for you," agreed Mary, and she ran happily toward the gun case. "This will be better than watching television." I should think so. Why watch some make-believe adventures when your own brother is preparing to shoot out the sides of your house? I put a quick stop to that. So did Lee. He suggested I clean the house. He said that he would bet the crickets would go to someone else's house. He said he was sure they didn't want to live in a place that had no crumbs or torn papers or gum wrappers or glass rings or dust.

Possibly he was right. I suppose they would have left if I had cleaned the windows, washed the curtains, and polished the floors. But I never did find out. I decided right away that I'd rather live with crickets than do all that. Besides, if Pinocchio could get used to it, certainly I could.

15

The Truth
about Family Camping

"Camping?" I wailed, when Lee brought home our first tent and proudly laid it out on the living room floor. "Who, me?"

"All of us," he declared firmly, and with a special look in my direction he announced that if he were expected to take a family the size of ours on any kind of an affordable vacation it would have to be taken in a tent or not at all. There was no way out.

"How soon?" I asked hopefully. "When the children are grown-up and married, perhaps?" Lee said that was NOT what he had in mind. It seems that he had been waiting for some of our family to be in junior high and old enough to rough it and help with things like driving stakes, gathering wood, and shoveling trenches, that this was the year and that was that. I stomped around the room for about five minutes, looking put-upon, and then told him he could take the tent out and show it to us, but that didn't mean I liked the idea.

The four older children were as enthusiastic about the whole thing as their father was, and Mary, the family messenger, had sprinted off at top speed to inform the neighbors that Daddy had brought home a new tent and that we were going camping on our vacation if Mommy didn't get a divorce. Amy was crawling on the kitchen cupboards rummaging for cookies to take with her to eat the minute we left, and Claudia sat quietly in the corner sucking her thumb.

I coyly suggested the younger children take the nice tent

into the back yard, put it out by the doghouse, and spend the rest of the day playing cowboys and Indians. "It will be fun," I said. "Just think, your very own private teepee."

"Tents are not toys," Lee said, drawing himself up with patient dignity. "And until we thoroughly understand all there is to know about it and learn each piece by name and where it goes, we will not put our tent up . . . it is going to be our 'home away from home' and FOR GOD'S SAKE DON'T STEP ON IT!" he shouted as I started to walk across the room to get an ashtray. I don't know how he thought I was going to cross over without stepping on it, for it covered the entire floor. Personally, I thought stepping on it had some advantages over dropping burning ashes on it, but I didn't want to say so. Lee was beginning to sweat and look cross. A bad sign.

The tent was a nauseous blue in color, and slept eight by advertisement. It was going to have to sleep nine by necessity, I pointed out. "Don't forget Augie," John said, pulling the dog close to his heart. "I don't want to leave Augie at home."

"I won't sleep with a dog," Karen said primly. I was with her. Ordinarily Augie slept with the boys . . . right in the middle. I had to agree with Karen—I didn't care to sleep with Augie either, nor did I particularly want to go camping with him. I didn't particularly want to go camping with anyone.

"We'll take Augie, all right," Lee said, his voice trembling with emotion. "He'll be our watch dog. You can't be too careful out in the wilderness." I immediately visualized being eaten by tigers, pounced on by panthers, and mauled by bears. I knew, deep in my heart, Augie was a chicken-dog. I made a mental note to sleep with a hatchet under my pillow for protection. I would chop at the first weird noise and ask questions later.

"The tent looks pretty hard to put up, if you ask me," I said, bending down to get a closer look at the hefty mass of canvas. I couldn't imagine that anything that could lay there so dormant and dumpy could possibly be converted into a "three-room house," as Lee claimed it could, without at least someone's having a master's degree in engineering.

"It's simple," he said, "but we have to learn all about it. That's the secret. Familiarity." And we spent the better part of the afternoon and evening learning by rote every single, solitary piece of that tent. Lee invented a game. He would call out a part of the tent, and the rest of us ran to identify it. The first one there was declared the winner. I held my own during the "flap, floor, and frame" portion, but faltered a little on "guy lines," and when he shouted "grommet" I was completely stunned. It sounded dirty to me. I suppressed the urge to yell "saute" and concentrated on learning the proper names for the proper places. Little did I know that before our vacation was over I would become intimately acquainted with every grommet on that tent. But I didn't know it then, and as I watched Lee and the boys plump the tent back into its canvas bag, the idea of camping suddenly didn't sound so bad. No telephones, no doorbells, no arguments over my makeup mirror, no vacuum cleaners, no television cartoons, no banging screen doors . . . peace and quiet under shady trees by lazy lakes with family togetherness. The Lord knew we were having trouble with any kind of togetherness since some of the children were going into junior high. This could be just the thing we needed most. To get reacquainted. To get our perspective as a happy, nuclear family back in gear. You see, I had been taken in by the advertisements, where Mama lounged in front of the tent in a flowered hostess gown, elegantly turning the spit with roast duckling and sipping a Manhattan while the kiddies played in organdy profusion beneath her feet and Papa chopped down the old sequoia for tomorrow's firewood. Lee flattened that dream by telling me he certainly expected me to cut down on the luggage by sharing suitcases.

"There's no way these children will share a suitcase," I told him. "Remember? We are dealing with the same children that have not cheerfully shared anything, including their parents, since they were six weeks old. I don't know how you expect me to get them to share suitcases." And I didn't know how he expected me to put seventy-five pounds of clothing into a nine-by-four-and-a-half-by-four-inch wee case which weighed one pound and cost $6.49—without taxes. But he did.

"I will not put my good blouse in the same suitcase as *hers*," Mary said, pointing at Susan. "Her stuff stinks." Susan was fourteen going on a sensational thirty-six, and she had been buying the strongest and strangest cologne marketed in the dime store for the past three months. I was well aware that any suitcase which held her clothes would have to be watched closely, as it surely would possess enough power on its own to hop out of the car and hitchhike out of the country. "And I won't put my things in with *theirs*, either," she said, pointing an accusing finger at John and David. I told her the boys' clothes wouldn't smell like perfume. "But they smell like skunks and old worms." She began to cry. "Why can't I have my own suitcase?" I told her to ask her dad, and I promised to launder everything thoroughly before we packed. Twice if necessary. And I kept my promise.

For many days before we left I washed and washed. And for many days before we left they dirtied and dirtied. As fast as I folded clothes into neat little piles and stacks, they wore them. Sons who hadn't changed socks since school ended suddenly insisted on four pairs of pure ones a day. Daughters who had worn the same cut-offs until they were stiff and gray-brown wouldn't answer the door or telephone without clean jeans. I couldn't wash fast enough to keep up with them. It was like a tribal fetish. But I couldn't wash away the fact that some of our clothes were fat. Lee said he could fix that, and with tremendous swiftness unpacked everything I had laboriously folded and packed in the suitcases. He squeezed and shoved them into place and said that he was trying to see that our luggage didn't weigh more than the car. He said at the rate we were going we were not going to be able to turn corners because the top of the car was heavier than the bottom. I thought he was exaggerating. I couldn't see where ten suitcases, eight sleeping bags, one cot, fourteen pillows, a satin comforter, three coolers, sixteen library books, a toy chest, and a thermos would cause that much of a problem. It wasn't my fault there was no room for the golf clubs and the tent. I didn't sit down and plan it out that way. I offered to leave a book or two behind.

Lee and I ended up sharing a suitcase, and on down the

line . . . Susan and Karen, John and David, Mary and Amy. I gave Claudia a paper sack. Most of her clothes were disposable anyway, and she didn't mind. She would be content with her thumb and an old chicken bone, so packing for her was no real problem, and Lee was happy. We had four suitcases and a paper sack. He eyed that sack with interest, but I put my foot down. I refused to put my double-knits in a paper sack and told him he could forget that idea right now. No one was going to see me traveling around the country carrying a brown paper bag with a red smiley face on it. It was bad enough I had to live in a tent.

The very first night we camped, I woke with the feeling of Tent brushing up against my cheekbone as its sides bulged in and out with the wind. The outside sounded dark and wild and raging as the wind built up to a maximum and my courage went down to a minimum. Frightened out of my wits, I kept repeating over and over, "The Tent is sturdy. The Tent has guy-wires and grommets. The Tent is safe. The Tent is my home-away-from-home." But down deep I knew the Tent knew it wasn't our permanent home and that it knew sooner or later its fickle family would abandon it to a corner in the garage and go back to living in carnal comfort in brick, stone, and wood. Would it try for an early revenge? I picked up the flashlight by my cot and threw the light over my sleeping family. "Please be awake, someone. I am lonely. And I am scared. And I want someone to talk to." I was even willing to talk to Claudia, who had a vocabulary of about four words and a grunt. No one moved. The children were tangled up like so many puppies and Lee was stretched out in the middle of the tent, his arms folded neatly over his chest like a corpse. He was snoring, so I knew he wasn't dead. The tent began to shudder and fold in the center with gusts and hard rain as bright flashes of lightning dashed in and out of my satin comforter, causing my spine to adhere to my cot like it was glued, and my hand to inch forward under my pillow for the hatchet. I had no idea what I would do with the hatchet, but its sharp presence made me feel a little more secure.

Above the sounds of the storm I could hear the brook trout flopping for their lives in the rushing creek located exactly three feet from the front of the tent. No doubt they were drowning in flood water, I thought, and it would be up to me to rescue my entire family before they were washed down the creek on green foam, snugly zipped up in their sleeping bags. Trembling, I crept from the cot and peered out the front flap of the tent. It was awful. Rain was coming down in sheets, whitecaps appeared on the creek, and I heard long, low moaning above the wind. A wandering camper caught beneath a tree branch? Someone from up the park sweeping by in the water? Someone struck by lightning? I listened closely and tried to remember how to give mouth-to-mouth.

"Yip! Yip!" the moan said. Why, it was poor Augie-Doggie. There goes the mouth-to-mouth, I said to myself, but nevertheless I couldn't let him drown or be whipped away by the wind. If the rest of us were going to go, the good-old-family-dog might as well go with us, and I prepared to leave the tent and rescue him. The tent gave a low heave as I grabbed one of its grommets and felt my way through the darkness. Augie showed his gratitude for my brave company by looking and smelling like a wet sheep and putting both paws on my shoulders and nuzzling his wet head into my nightgown and licking my neck. By the time we lunged back into the tent, I, too, was wet, cold, and smelled like a ram.

"Wake up!" I blew a cold, sheepy breath into Lee's ear and ran frozen fingers over his face.

"What the hell!" he bellowed, sitting straight up, his eyes closed tight and his hair sticking out in every direction, arms flapping up and down. "What's happening?"

"We are going to drown," I said calmly. "And I wanted to tell you good-bye and that I love you very much."

"We're not going to drown," he assured me, laying his now-wet head back on his sleeping bag. "Go back to your cot, go to bed, and go to sleep."

"I can't. I'm soaked and I'm cold and I'm scared." He suggested I put on dry clothes and relax. "I can't put on dry clothes," I told him. "Augie is sitting on our suitcase."

"Oh, Lord, move him and get some sleep." And he turned over and started to snore. He didn't ask how I got wet or how Augie happened to be inside the tent sitting on a suitcase or anything . . . he just closed his eyes and went to sleep. When the sun came up and the birds came out, I also closed my eyes and went to sleep for about forty-five seconds. Do you have any idea how early birds get up? Or how many there are in a forest? Thus began our first whole week of camping.

First Day. Karen accidentally placed the frying pan on Claudia's thumb, burning the skin completely off and causing her to scream very loud, me to scream very loud, and Karen to sob even louder. Campers rushed from miles around to see what had happened. The Park Ranger kindly suggested we see a doctor, and he patted Claudia gently on the head, me on the back, and Karen on the arm. Other campers murmured sympathetically, offering aid and comfort. Claudia was smothered in attention, and reacted accordingly by biting the doctor, located ten miles from the camp site. But he was nice and forgiving and gave her a sucker. She asked for six more to take back to brothers and sisters, and he smiled and obliged.

Second Day. David stepped on a broken bottle while fishing in the creek. He was barefooted and bled profusely. He screamed and I screamed and the camping crowd gathered again. The Park Ranger gave first aid, took Lee aside, and said he thought we should have David stitched up by the doctor and given a tetanus shot. We saw the doctor. He was still smiling and David returned to the camp, nine stitches richer, but with only one sucker.

Third Day. A tornado occured three miles south of our tent. I could see the tail of the twister sucking up objects and became hysterical, insisting that the whole family pile in the car, even though we were in the middle of lunch. Lee took one look at the canned spaghetti all over the interior of the car and became hysterical. I made everyone spend four hours huddled in the car until I was sure all danger had passed. We all became hysterical and John kept screaming this was the last time in his entire life that he would ever go on vacation with us again and I said, "Good." Lee grumbled and growled and other campers stood around our car, looking in at the crazy family locked up in a car, with all the windows up, fighting, while the sun was shining outside and the birds were singing and making messes on the Tent.

Fourth Day. Amy scooted under the protection fence to feed popcorn to the monkey in the park zoo. The monkey viciously chewed her little fingers instead of the popcorn and wouldn't let go until both boys had scampered over the fence and karate-chopped the monkey into submission. Lee was screaming obscene words at the monkey, Amy was screaming from fear and pain, and the rest of us were screaming just for the hell of it. The Park Ranger had set up camp near our tent and was there in a flash with his trusty little first aid kit and rotten advice. He was beginning to pale a little. Fellow campers were gathering in small groups, mumbling, pointing their fingers in our direction, and warning their children not to play with ours. We traveled ten miles to see our old friend, the doctor. He didn't smile and he didn't give Amy a sucker.

Fifth Day. Mary tripped over a rock in the dark and dented her head. I told the kids if they made one sound I would deck them. No need for everyone to know our business. The Park Ranger dragged out that silly box, visibly pale, and swore a little. I didn't take Mary to the doctor. I told Lee that I wouldn't take a child of mine to that stingy old thing.

Sixth Day. Susan took a quick tour of the nearby mountain range, falling down the entire distance on her head. We stood helplessly at the bottom as she plummeted down, bouncing from rock to rock. A very, very pale Park Ranger picked her up and laid her at my feet. I nearly fainted, and Lee sat on a log with his head between his legs. The other campers had not even come out of their tents. Susan giggled happily at her adventure and had to be threatened not to do the whole thing over again.

Seventh Day. The Park Ranger was the first one to our tent in the morning. He even beat the birds. He advised that perhaps we break camp and start for home. A roar of approval sounded from the crowd gathered before our tent. For once old P.R. and I were in complete agreement. Lee took one look at the surly crowd, the Park Ranger, who had developed a twitch. and our battle-scarred children and said, "Let's go home!" I was the first one in the car. Augie was second.

How marvelous it was to pull into our driveway and go back to our television, the doorbell, vacuum cleaner, and the telephone and a bathroom . . . a bathroom gloriously equipped with hot and cold running water, shiny chrome, and waxy tile—where I didn't have to watch for spiders.

16

High Class
Hotel Living Turned Sour

When Karen came home and cried that she was the only person in the entire junior high school who had never stayed overnight in a motel or slept on a water bed, Lee made the grand announcement that when the next four-day weekend came along we would take a trip and leave the tent at home and we would stay in a motel. I nearly passed out in delight. He didn't promise a water bed, however, but told her that would have to be something she did on her own. She was willing to compromise and I danced gaily out of the kitchen into the garage, where I stopped to pat the tent on its canvas back and say, "Sorry, fellow, you can't go along. We're going first class this time." I thought how fine it would be to take a vacation, even a short one, without living in fear of being molested by bugs, beetles, and bears. I didn't know taking seven children into a motel would be like pulling the plug in a bathtub: everything running out at the same time—money, dignity, clean towels, and the good family name. Gone . . . all gone . . . just like that.

After two hours out of town, there had been fourteen potty stops, three fist fights, one flat tire, and a couple of threats to find foster homes for each child. Lee began looking for a motel with the lowest rates. I watched for the nicest restaurants with bedrooms attached, and the children hunted for swimming pools. They didn't care if the entire motel was rat-infested as long as it had a swimming pool. An immediate swim became more important than punching each other out in the back seat.

"If I don't get to swim soon," David complained, "I won't be here for supper. You can just count me out."

"God," Karen sputtered. "John is breathing on me, Augie is sitting on my stomach, and Claudia has stuck a sucker in my hair. I will die if I don't get to clean up and have a swim."

"I'm going to be sick," Mary warned.

"I can't stand this," Susan said, and Amy began to cry because everyone was fighting. Lee pulled into the first available motel that had a swimming pool. He didn't worry about the rates, and I didn't worry about restaurants. Who worries about trivia? It was the most expensive and deluxe motel in the neighborhood, and the innkeeper was very rude. He acted as if it were not an everyday occurrence to have a station wagon littered with wretched, sweaty children, a dog in need of a pit stop, a crabby mother, and a near-hysterical father who had driven the past two hundred miles with a swim fin stuck in his ear pull up under his fancy red-and-white awning. The innkeeper sighed and said he could give us a kennel for Augie and two adjoining rooms for the nine of us. "Or you could rent the ballroom," he backhanded, pinching his lips together.

"Are the rooms poolside?" I asked in my I-have-stayed-in-the-best-motels-in-the-country-and-don't-mess-with-me-buddy voice. He laughed cheerfully and said, "No!" And he was right. Our rooms were located three flights and one-hundred and nine rooms away, and in order to swim we had to walk through the dining room, lobby, and cocktail lounge. Lee said he'd stay in the lounge. The innkeeper gave him three complimentary tickets for a free drink. "Ordinarily," he said, clutching Lee's hand, "we only give one, but I think I'll make an exception in your case."

Lee mumbled something about getting Augie settled in the kennel while I unpacked, and the children and I started for our rooms. The dining room was empty, thank goodness, when we passed through, but the lounge was full. I dragged John off a bar stool and side-stepped a pinch from a lecherous eighty-five-year-old gentleman who wore no teeth and had trembling hands. We made our alplike way to our rooms, which were light and airy and had only two towels in each of the bathrooms. I phoned for more towels and ignored the nastiness in the innkeeper's voice when he grudgingly promised to accommodate me. Claudia was delighted with the motel rooms. They were the first she had ever seen. She immediately packed the Gideon Bibles, motel stationery, telephone directories, and small soaps in her paper sack, and I immediately made her put them back. John and David were hanging out the windows yelling at passersby. Mary had turned on all the lights, the radio, and the television. Amy was playing horsie on the luggage racks; and Karen and Susan were in separate bathrooms trying on each other's bathing suits. Lee came back from putting Augie in the kennel with a happy, lopsided smile on his face. "This is a fine vacation," he said. "Let's all go swimming."

Motel swimming pools are usually limited in size, and this particular one was doubly so. It was fine for the honeymoon couple wanting to take an early morning dip, or elderly grandparents who wished to do nothing more than sit on the side of the pool and get smashed, or tiny, small-boned people with one preschooler.

It was obviously not built for our family. I wanted to go back and complain to the snotty innkeeper about his puny pool, but Lee wouldn't let me because he said the innkeeper was a fine fellow and I should leave him alone. I discovered his attitude had something to do with the fact he had cashed in all three complimentary tickets at the bar in fifteen minutes and also had had a quick one with a nice old fellow who was a real gentleman and scholar but a little difficult to understand because he had no teeth. He'd even taken the old gentleman's name and address . . . thought he'd be a great companion for Auntie-dear.

"Take turns going in," I whispered to the children as we approached the side of the pool. "For God's sake don't all jump in at the same time. The water will come out over the edges and they will sue us or throw us out. That innkeeper is just waiting for the chance. Don't give it to him."

David, who felt the Olympics had made a mistake when they hadn't picked him for competition at the age of nine, did a nifty swan dive in the shallow end of the pool that was clearly labeled No Diving; John shoved Mary into the six-foot side, causing her to scream bloody murder, scaring the grandparents with the scotch and water out of their wits; Susan hopped into the hot sauna, scalding her entire body; Amy and Claudia wandered into the bar to find Auntie-dear's new boyfriend; and Karen had quietly stretched out for a sun bath in direct view of the rock band that was to appear in the lounge that evening. Lee instantaneously threw a beach towel over Karen, gave the rock band a father's no-nonsense look, tweaked David's ear, thumped John's head, rescued a screaming Mary (who swam like a fish but liked the dramatic), and offered to buy the jolted grandparents another round—saying he'd join them, of course.

I took a water-dripping, lobsterlike Susan by the hand and picked up the two little girls in the bar and sailed through the dining room, completely full by now, dribbling on menus and ruining appetites, and returned to our room, vowing never to leave it again until it was time to go home.

"But we have to eat," Lee said, trying to bribe me to leave the room by hitting in the spot he knew I was weakest.

"Order room service," I suggested.

"For nine people? Not on your life. Augie's the only one that gets room service this trip. The rest of us eat in the dining room or not at all."

Naturally I gave in. I had eaten every peanut, cracker, and sucker we had brought along in the car and knew it wouldn't sustain me through the night. I was going to have to face the dining room and the hoity-toity innkeeper.

"Try to keep it under two dollars each," I told the children. "You don't have to order the most expensive dish on the menu. We aren't made of money." David automatically craved the most costly item on the menu whenever he entered a restaurant. Even now, I have a hard time convincing him ordinary people don't eat steak and lobster for breakfast, especially when Dad picks up the check.

"And don't get up and run around looking for the bathroom, don't giggle, don't eat with your fingers, don't shuffle your feet, slurp your soup, or duel with your salad forks. In other words—mind your manners!" I barked.

"Maybe the dining room will be empty," Lee dreamed.

"Don't count on it," I said. The place was full of people, and like a wagon train crossing the Old West Trail, the nine of us filed behind the hostess. I felt like shouting,

"Hamburger ho!" as we weaved among the diners, but remembering the rules, I pulled myself together. We were taken to an obscure table partially hidden by a giant artificial green fern. John complained that the plastic fern fronds kept dipping into his water glass and I suggested he need not cause a scene, just move the glass.

My optimism of $2 per plate, per child, was short-lived. "If I stick to that," old rare-meat-and-tail said, "I'll get one toothpick and a side order of pickle relish. I can't live on that." I told David I didn't expect him to, and asked Amy to quit fiddling with the fern.

"Let's go buffet," Lee suggested. It was over the limit, but probably the best we could do, and it would eliminate putting the poor confused waitress through fourteen order changes. Anyway, I loved buffets. I loved hovering and yearning over the varieties of salads, vegetables, and desserts, and the challenge of placing the food on my plate and the suspense of wondering if there would be enough room for the roast beef and ham at the end of the line.

"Can we go back for seconds?" David shivered in anticipation as we passed through the buffet line.

"No, take it now or not at all," I said, and looked at his plate. It resembled the Tetons, and he hadn't even reached the vegetables. "You don't need four rolls," I snapped. "Pass three of them to your sisters." People were staring. I'm sure they were wondering if this particular child had ever sat down to a full meal before.

Somewhere in the line and the mix-up Amy had gotten sidetracked—or lost. She came back to the table with a tear on her cheek and one small radish on her plate. "I couldn't reach anything," she sobbed. "This is all I could get. That lady over there dropped it." I nodded politely to our grandmotherly-looking lady from the pool and pushed Amy's empty plate in front of Lee.

"You go fill it," I whispered.

"I've been there once and I just sat down," he whispered back. "I don't want to go back again. The innkeeper is watching."

"I'll do it," David volunteered, "if I can have half." I talked Karen into helping her little sister. I told her it would be good practice for her, as she would become a mother some day. She said she certainly would never have any children. But she did. Two. But that's another story.

Eventually we settled down to the business of eating. The steady hum of customer conversation in the dining room blacked out the steady crunch from our table as three of the children played "rabbit" with their celery down at their father's end of the table. He said they weren't hurting a soul and at least they were sitting still. I decided not to rock the boat and concentrated on my whipped potatoes and gravy. I felt a tap on my shoulder. It was the grandmotherly lady from across the room. "My God, she wants her radish back," I thought. Too bad, David had eaten it long ago with his fourth roll.

"I just want to tell you," she said. "I've been watching you all day." Oh, Lord! "Such a fine family. So mannerly. How proud you must be." I looked about the table and sixteen eyes looked back at me. I smiled. "I am," I said. "Very proud. Thank you very much."

I only hoped she hadn't seen the chicken leg sticking out of David's pocket.

THERE GOES MY OPINIONS, MY MONEY, MY PEACE OF MIND, AND MY CAR

Senior High Stage

17

Driving a Garbage Can

As the children entered senior high school, I surrendered my opinions, my money, my peace of mind, and my car. The car went first, and the other things followed in rapid succession. I didn't attend a White House reception or have two sailors fight over me in a bar or be interviewed by a private detective or pose for a centerfold or smoke strange things, but that didn't mean this period of my life was dull. On the contrary, my life reached a level of excitement that can only be compared to buckling yourself into the copilot's side of a jet airliner for a lark and having the pilot pass away quietly as the plane approaches the dead-ahead view of the Rocky Mountains. Lee gave me permission to teach the children to drive.

"It will be better if you do it," he explained. "You won't be so critical, because you drive funny yourself. You won't know what's going wrong so you won't yell so much and you won't get so upset." I said, "Thank you," and went into the closet and cried. I didn't think I was going to like being dropped down into the center of traffic with someone whose coordination skills still included tripping over the evening paper as it lay on the floor. One or two learned to drive like their dad—strong, solid, and safe. One or two like me— erratic, spontaneous, and down the middle of the road, and one or two drove like no one else in this world before them.

I cowered in the corner of the passenger side of our car when Karen learned, and Lee insisted he would go with her when she was thirty years old but not a day before. John and David declared they would never ride with her, even if they had to walk to the swimming pool for the rest of their lives. Susan said she'd go anywhere with anyone, just so it didn't include school, and the three little girls played "crash" with their Barbie doll cars, putting Ken into traction and Karen into tears. I told her not to cry, that her dad wouldn't ride with me, either, and who wanted to take the boys anywhere, anyway? I certainly didn't want to, and some day, I assured her, they would all want to learn to drive, too, and she'd be the only one with a license and then she could wave her very own personal set of car keys in their faces and have the last laugh. She dried her tears, shrugged her shoulders, and said it didn't matter, she'd get her boyfriend to teach her. Lee turned on his fatherlike heels and shouted she knew damn good and well she couldn't date anyone over sixteen and sixteen-year-olds couldn't legally teach sixteen-year-olds to drive and if that one boy in the tight pants and granny glasses who looked old enough to maneuver a semi rang our doorbell one more time or called after ten o'clock the police would be notified. Somehow the subject of teaching Karen to drive never came up again after that, and somehow she learned. Of course for a while she shifted gears with a vengeance, had a heavy foot, and called me "Good buddy," but I didn't ask questions.

When I rode with Susan, I sat quietly beside her with my eyes shut. She drove with one finger and one of God's guardian angels sitting on her shoulder. "You have two hands and ten good fingers," I said. "Please use them!" And I inched closer to the door handle, preparing to jump out as she waved to friends, combed her hair, fiddled with her charm bracelet, adjusted the rear view mirror, pawed through her purse, and twirled the steering wheel like a baton with her forefinger. "My driver's ed teacher says I'm the best in the class," she said proudly. "He isn't nervous like you are, Mom."

John, a perfectly fine young man in all respects, turned evil the minute he had a wheel in his hands. He drove the car like a cement mixer. "If I race the motor before I leave the driveway," he said, "I know it will make it out onto the street." He demonstrated by turning on the key, placing his foot on the accelerator, and pushing off with all his might. Blue smoke and a roar filled the air. Augie flew off the porch and down the sidewalk, birds left the treetops, and squirrels dropped their nuts. The car vibrated for five minutes. I vibrated for ten. "It gets the cobwebs out of the engine," he

118

shouted over the noise as we raced an Airedale down the street, picking up speed at the intersection and soaring by the football field with our nose to the ground and the rear end of the car standing straight up.

"You can't go this fast," I squealed. "You'll get us both thrown in jail."

"I'm only going twenty-five," he said, and looking at the speedometer, I saw that he was right. Why did it feel like a hundred and twenty-five?

"It's because he is only sixteen," Lee said. "You are going to have to learn to relax more, Shirley, when you are out with him in the car. You'll make him a fidgety driver if you continue to be such a nag."

David bypassed automobiles altogether and went straight to a motorcycle. I couldn't stand that, and I wouldn't ride on it, either. "You'll never get me on that thing," I screamed as David tore out of the yard and around the corner. "The next thing we know he'll have spikes on his shoes and wear black leather underwear." Lee looked envious, and I wondered how in the world I would ever launder black leather underwear, but I didn't have to worry. A giant eighteen-wheeler solved the motorcycle problem by racing David on the highway, splashing him with mud, and sucking off his hubcaps. He rapidly sold the motorcycle and stood in line for his turn at the family car. I made his helmet into a planter.

Mary drove as if she was performing a ballet. She swerved and dipped and tippy-toed and bowed and slowly side-stepped as she attempted to parallel park. Cars backed up behind her for three blocks. "Don't you think you should park closer to the curb instead of staying out here in the mainstream of traffic?" I suggested timidly. I tried to keep the concern out of my voice because I didn't want her to cry.

"Don't bug me," she replied, a tear gathering in the corner of her eye.

"I don't think we should have one wheel on the sidewalk." I gritted my teeth. "I think we should move out as quickly and as quietly as we can." We were dangerously close to entering a nearby drugstore . . . via the window.

"Don't bug me," she said, tears slipping down her cheeks.

"A lot of cars are honking at us."

"You're bugging me." And she broke into loud, racking sobs, fogging the windshield. I turned on the defroster so she could see through the mist, and suggested she get us home as soon as possible. To this day Mary doesn't parallel park. As far as that goes, neither do I.

I suspicioned that Amy might have picked up the ability to drive when she was about two years old by watching television (or her brother John), for when I took her out for her first lesson she said, "I already know that," and executed maneuvers only seen on major high-speed law-enforcement chases or ambulance runs. When I turned chalk-white and hyperventilated, she told me she knew what she was doing and proved it by driving my car everywhere. She no longer used her legs except to walk to the telephone and the refrigerator. She drove the car with the gas tank on empty and the tires without air, and got where she was going and back without incident. The car began to spend seventy-five percent of its time hiked up on the grease rack while a repair man with creased brows wondered how the motor turned over with pom-poms draped over its innards. Amy closed the ashtrays, gunned the motor, and drove happily through high school.

Claudia moved a little slower. She was about four or five years old before she showed a distinct interest in getting her driver's license. "This year, Mommy?" she asked. "No, not this year," I told her. "You must learn to read first."

"Now?" She was eight and was having trouble roller skating.

"Not now," I put her off.

"I'm ready," she announced when she was twelve. And she was, for each day after, until she was old enough for a permit, she X-ed the days off on the calendar.

"You cannot drive and disco at the same time," I told her when she was finally ready and we were hustling out into the street for the first time. Her shoulder was wiggling, her head bobbing up and down, and her foot keeping time on the gas pedal. "Concentrate on what you are doing and forget the BeeGees."

"But I love the BeeGees," she said.

"They are not paying for the gas," I pointed out. "If we must have music while we drive, find something soft or symphonic." She flipped off the radio, said she couldn't drive at all now, and that she really did wish she had someone to teach her who wasn't so nervous. "Why did I have to be the youngest?" she said wistfully. "Everyone yells at me, I have to wear hand-me-downs, and I miss out on everything."

This, of course, was not true. According to her older sisters and brothers, we made them wait until they were in their early twenties before trusting the family car to them. "I had to buy my own car," Karen said. "And furnish the gas, the taxes, and pay my own telephone bills." David claimed he didn't dare ask for our car until he was twenty-two and had spent four years in college proving to us that he was stable enough to drive, and Amy was insulted to think that Claudia was allowed to carry a set of car keys to a car that she obviously thought of as her own but was registered in my name.

I was really afraid that a conscientious sanitary crew would haul the car away during our town's annual clean-up week when they promised to remove, free of charge, refuse, broken bedsprings, abandoned refrigerators, trash bags, scrap iron, old furniture, and general junk and debris.

"I am tired of driving a garbage can." I was annoyed and I showed it. "We are going to clean the car and KEEP IT CLEAN! I don't even like to drive to the grocery store. It's embarrassing when the carry-out boy can't find a place to put the grocery sacks because of all the rubble. Last week I had to put the frozen food between my legs to drive home." Lee hid a chuckle behind his hand and John sighed in a typical teen-aged tormented manner and said, "It's not that bad, Mother, you're exaggerating again."

"Mothers don't lie," I told him. "Yesterday, I sat on a Dilly Bar stick covered with chocolate, poked my foot into three inches of gum wrappers, couldn't see out of the rear view mirror because of the jackets piled in the back seat, crunched fourteen yellow M & M's with my left heel, scratched my elbow on eight pairs of sunglasses, and had to fight my way through three months of homework to find the radio. And you tell me I'm exaggerating! Why, I even found an empty beer can scrunched under the front seat. Can you explain that?" John didn't say another word. I knew he wouldn't.

It wasn't always that way. I can remember when Lee and I were dating. The car he drove, though old, was as neat as a pin. Road maps were in alphabetical order and folded with sharp precision. The whisk broom had a special place all its own and could be picked up and applied with swift strokes if so much as a molecule of dust entered the car. The rubber mats were black and bright and I could reach my hand underneath the seats to retrieve a dime without fear of having it snapped off by a unidentifiable creature lurking in dark recesses. We could actually see out of the windows, every single one of them. But as our family grew, so did the pile of sucker sticks around the foot feed.

"Everyone is equally responsible," I said, "and everyone is going to help clean the car." I handed out rags, sprays, brooms, and hefty plastic bags. "Clean!" I ordered. No one was exempt. Even Augie had to bury the bones he had stashed between the seat belts.

It wasn't too long before the car looked fit for a regal family. It was shining. Even the speedometer looked younger. A truly magnificent sight. "I'm going to the grocery store, and I can't wait to see the expression on that carry-out boy's face when I drive up in this." I was so proud. No corn dog sacks, no gym socks, no ribbons or mittens, no chewed-up sunflower seeds in paper cups, no straws to poke my eyes out when I turned a corner. It was a triumphant moment. Short-lasting, perhaps, but long enough for me to wallow in and savor for as long as possible. Hopping into the car happily, I turned the key in the ignition and waited, expecting to hear the hum of a tidy, contented motor. Nothing. I slammed down on the accelerator and shifted the gears into Drive. Silence. I jammed my stomach into the steering wheel. Deadlock. I muttered four fairly obscene words under my breath. Noiseless. I screamed four very obscene words out loud. Zip. Rushing into the house, I shouted, "The car won't start. The car won't start!" And I stood in the middle of the kitchen and wept.

"Don't cry, Mom," David said. "I'll fix it." He took a bag of crushed potato chips, a box of taco shells, four hairbrushes, a beat-up lunch box, a thermos bottle, and pair of tennis shoes and threw them into the car, leaving smudges on the windows as he did so.

"Now try it," he said. I hesitated, turned the key, stepped on the starter, and do you know . . . that silly car hummed and purred like a kitten.

18

Of Course I Can Ride a Bike, It's as Easy as Sex

When the children took over my car I announced to everyone that I was going to buy a bicycle. No fanfare. No theatrics. No dramatics. Just a simple statement. "I am going to buy a bicycle." Everyone laughed. Except Karen. She burst into tears. "Oh God, Mom! Are you going to ride it in public?"

"Of course I am going to ride it in public. There is very little room in the kitchen." I couldn't understand why it was such a shock to everyone. My body needed the exercise, my pocketbook needed the relief from its dozens of trips to the gas pumps, and my country needed my efforts to conserve energy. I was being healthy, wealthy, and patriotic all at one shot. And I never had the car anyway.

"Can you even ride a bicycle?" Lee asked.

"Naturally, I can ride a bicycle. Anyone can ride a bicycle. You never forget. It is like sex. Once you do it, the ability to do it again simply doesn't go away. It is a natural reflex." Lee continued to look doubtful. I'm not sure he was impressed with my natural reflexes or my sexual ability. He evidently had grim thoughts about my future on a bicycle, but he was a good sport and went along with it and told me he'd accompany me to the store and help me pick it out. The children wanted to go, too. Augie-Doggie ran to get his leash.

"Not you, dog," I said. "You aren't going. You stay here and answer the telephone."

Shirley Lueth

It took me a while to get dressed for the shopping trip because I didn't know what a person wore to buy a bicycle. I didn't think it could be just any old ordinary run-of-the-mill outfit. I had clothes to cook in, clothes to garden in, clothes to play golf in, clothes to go to dinner in, clothes to attend funerals, weddings, graduations, PTA, and church in, but I had nothing suitable to wear to buy a bicycle in. I had seen teen-agers wearing short shorts and halters when they rode their bikes, but I discarded that idea immediately for many obvious reasons. My jeans were too tight and polyester slacks didn't quite seem flashy enough. Lee stood in the doorway of our bedroom twiddling his thumbs and scowling. "It really doesn't matter what you wear," he said.

"I don't want the salesman to think I'm an amateur." I was well aware of the fact first impressions are important. Lee said if I wanted to buy and he had the cash, the salesman wasn't going to be interested in what I was wearing. He said the salesman would sell me a bicycle if I was wearing a nightgown. He certainly knew what he was talking about, because that salesman greeted me with open arms and a smile on his face that would've made Auntie-dear break out in goose pimples. I marched right up to him and said, "Show me your bicycles." I was wearing white slacks and a striped knit shirt. I thought I looked sporty and quite athletic. I don't think he noticed.

"For the children?" he leered, rubbing his hands together and mentally pedaling seven bicycles out the door.

"No, for me," I answered, and he tried to sell me a three-wheeler. "It's perfect for you," he said. "Just perfect. You can carry your groceries and everything." I wiggled my white slacks and flaunted my striped shirt. I pulled in my stomach and squared my shoulders. I flexed my calves and resisted the urge to hit him in the mouth. "No sir," I said in a deep, husky voice, "I want a bicycle bicycle. With two wheels."

"A ten-speed, I presume," he said, sarcasm dripping from his dentures. "With a banana seat?" Amy clapped her hands. She had visions of inheriting a brand new ten-speed when clumsy old mother broke her pelvis.

"I'm not going across country," I said. "I'm only going around the neighborhood. I want a regular bicycle with regular brakes, regular seat, regular pedals, and regular

124

handlebars." By now my face was flushed and my white slacks were drooping. Lee had disappeared into hardware, the younger children were hovering behind appliances, and the three older ones had left the store with the lame excuse that they wanted to ring up old Augie on the telephone. It was the salesman and me.

He showed me a slender-framed one with paper-thin tires. I knew that delicate piece of machinery wouldn't hold me up for more than three minutes. The salesman didn't argue when I rejected it. He brought out a chunky, midget-sized one with enormous handlebars. It looked like a dumpy, fat Texas Longhorn.

"My knees would hit my chin if I rode that." I wasn't getting anywhere with this stubborn man. "I absolutely don't want one like that." He wheeled out a blue bike with straight, sturdy crossbars. "That's a boy's bike," I gasped. "No." One false move and I could've been ruined for life. Finally I spied the perfect bicycle shoved in a corner. It had cobwebs in its spokes and it was heavy and tough and its tires were wide and thick. It was the type of bicycle no child would be caught dead on. It was just what I wanted. "I'll take that one!" I pointed to its rusty red frame. "And put that sweet little wicker basket with the daisies painted in the middle right on the handlebars." I planned to go first class. But I hadn't planned on riding it home from the store the very same day I bought it.

"But I have to practice," I told Lee as he paid the bill and told me to hop on my new bike and run on home. "I have to adjust the pedals and study hand signals. I think I should ease into it gradually . . . like riding it in the garage before I try it in public."

"Surely you don't need practice," he said, shoving his billfold in his back pocket. "Remember, you said anyone can ride a bicycle. You said it was second nature. You said you would never forget. You said it was as easy as sex."

"I lied."

"And," he continued, "there is no room for a bicycle in the back seat with all the children. You'll either have to ride it home or leave it here, and you can't do that because it's paid for."

I turned to each member of our family, hoping perhaps one of them would ride it home for me. No, they would not ride it home for me. In fact, they lined up outside on the sidewalk in front of the store so they wouldn't miss the take-off. The salesman was at the head of the line. He was as excited as the children. My moment of truth had come. I had to hitch my body up onto that bicycle in front of everyone and prove that I wasn't too old and too broken down to ride a two-wheeler. It had been about thirty years since I had ridden a bicycle and my legs seemed shorter. "Shouldn't I have a helmet?" I asked. "I have one at home. I can take the flower out."

"You don't need a helmet!" Lee said. "That's for motorcycles."

"Oh," I mumbled, my chin dropping in shame. I was stalling for time. "How far is to to our house? It's too far to ride a bicycle."

"Four blocks, and you start first. We'll follow in the car."

And pick up the pieces, I thought, as I threw one short leg over the seat the way I remembered doing when I was fourteen. A crunch in the knee-cap area told me my leg wasn't going to go all the way over. It seemed I was going to cripple myself the first two minutes of my athletic life. Changing my approach, I straddled the bicycle, put one foot on a pedal, shoved off with the other, and zipped down the sidewalk. Smoke must have been pouring from my tires as I felt the power of the bicycle beneath my body. "Get off the sidewalk," Lee yelled from the car, moving slowly beside me. "You can't ride a bicycle on the sidewalk."

"I can't get off the sidewalk. There are cars parked in the way." People had plastered their bodies to the storefronts as I peeled by, and were grabbing up little children. My choice was to plunge into the traffic and be smashed or take my chances on knocking off a pedestrian. "Watch out, watch out!" I shouted, and stayed on the sidewalk.

"Stop wobbling," Lee shrieked. "You're going to hit someone. People can't tell where you're going."

"Their problem," I thought, and continued to cause terror on the sidewalk as Lee held up traffic in the street. Soon, however, the terror ended and so did the sidewalk. I skimmed across the intersection and barely missed being crushed by two cars. Lee was driving one of them.

Down the street and around the corner I flew. A little dog barked and snapped at my spokes. An astonished friend met me eye to eye as I wheeled by. She was in her car and didn't expect to see me trucking by on a bicycle. In polite habit she put up her arm and waved. I nodded hello with great dignity. I couldn't raise my hand and wave back, for there was no earthly way I was going to remove one finger from the handlebar. I only had to hope she understood I wasn't being a snob just because I had a new bicycle. A spasm jogged my upper leg and traveled into my pelvic area, and my gallbladder and kidneys shivered. I hadn't remembered bicycling hurting so much.

"Pop a wheelie, Mom," John shouted as they pulled up beside me. Hello, wheelie. One rear-up of that bicycle and I would've been finished forever. Our house loomed ahead. Thank God, I was nearly home. If I could turn into the driveway, I could have a drink and go to bed. I narrowly missed the driveway, much like I did when I drove the car, and sliced through our neighbor's prize roses. I got an ankle full of thorns and scared a butterfly out of its wits, but I came home in one aching piece. Coming to rest on the steps of the front porch, narrowly missing being pitched through the front door, I asked my family, "Well, how did I do? How did old Mom do?"

"You looked a little like the witch on Wizard of Oz," Mary commented. "All you needed was Toto." I looked at Augie-Doggie. He turned and trotted away before I got any funny ideas. That dog wanted no part of me or my bicycle.

Oh well, he wouldn't fit into the little white basket anyway.

19

Where Does All the Money Go?

I knew the children were still around even when they were growing up. I could tell by the toothpaste smears on the walls and the occasional call from the local police department, but it wasn't a hand-touching, conversation-exchanging kind of contact. Just as I had grown used to living in a house with jelly on the woodwork, diapers in the washing machine, and tic-tac-toe on the windows, suddenly and dramatically the whole atmosphere of our home changed. It became morose, mute, and much too big. "It's so quiet in here," I complained to Lee as we settled down in the living room for a long evening at home . . . alone. "It's so calm, so boring. Nothing is going on. The house is like a tomb."

"Isn't it wonderful?" Lee laughed deliciously, stretching out before the television set as Monday night football romped uninterrupted across the screen. No one was fighting but the losing team's quarterback. No one was kicking and screaming but the cheerleaders, and no one was throwing anything but a football. No one was home.

Oh, they had been there, off and on, throughout the week. I could tell by the way the stereo panted in the corner from being overtweeted and overwoofed, its diamond needle on the verge of turning plastic from too much use. There were no potato chips, jelly doughnuts, Cokes, or frozen pizzas left anywhere. And there were one thousand six hundred and ninety-three schoolbooks, notebooks, annual pictures, jackets, sweaters, pencils, hairbrushes, combs, gym shorts, and paper sacks gathered daily in the middle of the dining room table. The shower foamed at the mouth with shampoo.

Here was a dirty flannel shirt with the pocket torn, a lone tennis shoe, a lint-covered Cert, a punched-out cafeteria ticket, and a yellow cloud of spray cologne hanging from the ceiling like smog. No, they had not left home completely . . . it was simply, now that they were growing up, we didn't meet face to face.

"It's like they were invisible." I placed my forehead on the side of the wall in frustration. "I see their remains but I never see them."

"I think I saw one of them thumbing through my billfold a couple of days ago," Lee said as he fixed me a toasted cheese sandwich to calm me down. "But I never see them," I sobbed between gulps of cheese and burnt bread. "I miss them. Don't you understand?"

"I understand this," he said, handing me the pickles and mustard and another cheese sandwich. "I remember when you used to say 'I can't wait until they all grow up!' " I didn't remember saying that. "And how you used to go on about being the only wife and mother in the neighborhood preparing banquet portions for every meal." I did remember saying that.

And even though no one was there I continued preparing banquet portions for every meal. I fixed food for nine people, but only three were showing up. Lee, Augie-Doggie, and me. And we were rapidly gaining weight because I couldn't bear to put three tablespoons full of peas in a pot. As far as I was concerned, if you couldn't throw in a couple of cans it wasn't worth turning on the stove. Faithfully, I fried twelve pork chops and mashed twelve potatoes. I expected eighteen feet under the family table, by God, and that's what I cooked for. And then the telephone messages came and handwritten notes appeared. "Will not be home to eat. Car in front of school if you need it. Out of gas. Will be home early." One had gone to play football, one had gone to play volleyball, one had gone to play at a friend's house, one had gone to play tennis, one had gone to play at a part-time job downtown, one had gone to play at babysitting, and one had gone to play at only heaven knew what. There would be four feet and four paws under our table, and I had prepared enough for fifteen. When I did get it all in proper perspective and learned to cook for two with a little left over for Augie, they all left home permanently, had families of their own, and began dropping in, unexpectedly, for breakfast, lunch, and dinner, and there we were . . . right back where I started, caught with my spatula down.

In the meantime we spent one million dollars on all the wrong clothes, watched our sons learn to shave without cutting their throats and our daughters grow pretty even though we had only one really good mirror in the house, shared by six females. By now, of course, I was approaching middle age and didn't want to look in a mirror anyway. I told Mary she could have my turn if she wanted it. She did and sold raffle tickets to her sisters for ten cents each for the privilege of winning that turn. I wish I had her financial ingenuity. I never had any money because I was methodically, efficiently, and cold-bloodedly dimed and dollared right out of every nickel I had. Our children could sniff out stray money at three hundred paces.

"Mom, I need a dollar," Susan would say once every fifteen minutes.

"What for?" I answered, not wanting to hand it out willy-nilly.

"I have to buy an eraser for school." This was known as the old school-supply squeeze. They all knew I was a push-over for anything educational.

"An eraser costs a dollar?" I puzzled. It didn't seem right to me. I was always under the impression that an eraser cost somewhere in the neighborhood of twenty-nine cents, plus tax. But I've been wrong before.

"I'll bring change," she said.

Somehow there never seemed to be any change. I was left at home sorting through couch cushions for stray pennies or quarters, which didn't seem to be any way for a grown-up mother to spend her time.

Occasionally I had a windfall. One day I had ten dollars left over after paying the paper boy. It was mine, by golly, and no one knew I had it. Not even Augie. The paper boy knew, but I hoped he'd keep his mouth shut. "I'm sending this to the poor little naked children in India," I explained, in case he had any doubts. "I'm going to put it in an envelope and mail it right away." I locked all the doors, pulled the drapes, turned off the lights, and sank down in a heap behind the big chair in the living room. I was partially hidden by a giant Boston fern and I was positioned so no one could see me. I took out my ten-dollar bill and fondled it. I smoothed out all the wrinkles and kissed the rather stern lips of Alexander Hamilton. "I love you," I whispered.

With the Boston fern tickling my neck, I spent a delightful afternoon caressing my money. Mr. Hamilton looked softer somehow, as the molestations and the day wore on. I think he was beginning to turn on.

David hit the porch from school about the time Alex and I were discussing a motel rendezvous, and I quickly slipped out from behind the chair and carefully stashed the ten dollars in my right shoe. I pressed my fingers over the fern, pinching his leaf ever so gently, and hissed, "If you say one word about my money, I'll drown you."

"Hi, Mom!" David called out as he came through the living room. "I need seven dollars for tube socks, and why are you talking to the flower?" And looking in the direction of my shoe, he added, "I smell something."

"It's good to talk to plants and you smell cookies. In the kitchen." A cookie in the jar is worth more than an unknown odor in the shoe, and he disappeared. I sat down, tucking the shoe with the money beneath me just as Karen opened the door.

"Did you have a good day, Mom? Can I have some money? Why are you sitting on your foot? You'll get cramps."

I was sure she didn't need the money. It was an automatic reflex when she saw her mother. I sent her to the kitchen with her brother. Susan came home, handed me her Want List, and after looking me over carefully and sniffing about a bit, she looked wistful and asked me to read it out loud so we could discuss her immediate needs. Her list included the inevitable eraser and eleven spiral notebooks.

"Why do you need so many spiral notebooks?" I asked. "I bought fourteen two days ago."

"I don't know," she said, tossing me one of her Why-do-you-ask-me-so-many-dumb-questions looks. "I just need them."

"Ask your dad for the money," I said in a cheap, determined voice. "He's the man with the belt." We all knew

Lee kept his money zipped in a belt. The children suspected he wore it to bed.

Lee was greeted at the door with a barrage of needs from Susan and David, and Karen stood around with her hand out, just in case money was passed around.

"I don't have any money," he said, clutching his waistline. "Ask your mother."

"She doesn't have any either," Susan said. "No one in this family ever has any money. I hate being poor." I wiggled my toes and kept my mouth shut.

"But I left twelve-fifty for the paper boy," Lee said, turning to look me straight in the eye. "The bill was only two-fifty. What happened to the change?"

"I'm sorry," I answered sweetly. "There wasn't any change." I may be middle-aged, but I can still use my head when I need to.

20

Fuzzy Fond Memories

There is no reasonable explanation why having teen-agers should whet the appetite. But it did, and the faster the children entered high school the faster I ate. I no longer had my preschool skittish skin-and-bones look sometimes associated with a mother when she has nothing to do all day but gun down toddlers; I gained weight in every available spot on my body, including hips, chin, and the backs of my knees. I dieted religiously and became very irritable, impatient, and demanding.

"How can you possibly marry with a clear conscience if you can't make a decent bed?" I severely reprimanded Karen when she was sixteen.

"I'm going to have servants," she said with confidence. "I won't have to make beds or peel potatoes or sweep under stoves and I will probably adopt all of my children. I will marry a rich man."

"That's nice," I said, planning to move in with her when she did. "But in the meantime, you are living with your underprivileged parents and it's time you accepted the responsibility of making your own bed in this house every single day . . . starting right now."

"I will. Just give me time."

So I gave her time. I gave her four telephone calls (one hour each), three trips to the nearest drive-in, six changes of clothing, and eight soap operas. "Now it is time to make your bed," I insisted. Karen called it nagging. She told me it was time to go to bed and how silly it was to make a bed right before a person hopped into it. I couldn't argue with that.

When I told the boys to make their beds, John explained patiently that bachelors didn't make their own beds or clean their rooms, and that when and if he did get married his wife would do all the work so why should he learn. Lee gave him a funny look.

Now, despite what our children might tell you, Lee and I didn't marry and have children in order to provide ourselves with in-house handmaidens and errand boys. If I had planned that, I would've picked another bunch. I wouldn't have chosen a daughter who collapsed with stomache pains because I asked her to stir the soup or a son who broke out in hives because he had to carry a couple of card table chairs across a ten by twelve room, or a daughter who looked at me with great tears in her eyes and said, "You hate me," when I handed her a dish towel instead of my car keys, or anyone who wanted to eat in the living room and let Augie lick the dishes instead of stacking them in the dishwasher. Any mother worth her cookbook knows it is easier to do it herself than it is to depend on a child. Unless this child is one who has been pressed carefully between the pages of a book like a wildflower and only taken out on occasion to show off to friends and relatives.

"It's for your very own good," I told them. "If you don't learn at home, where will you learn?" John said he thought he could order a magazine that came in a plain brown wrapper that might have a section in it on housekeeping for the single man. I told him I wouldn't have him looking at those magazines, let alone reading them. Amy said he already had some, because she had found them under his mattress and taken one to school for "Show and Tell" and the teacher had turned red in the face and left the room and she saw her talking to the school principal and I said, "Oh, my God," and dropped the subject. Lee told me it was natural for young boys to have a healthy interest in such glossy photographs and no, our son wasn't a pervert and yes, he would marry a nice girl some day. It was none of my business, he further informed me whether he, himself, had looked at pictures like that at a young age or an old age. Didn't I tell him once that husbands were only little boys with a paycheck and big shoes? I shouldn't misunderstand, he continued; I was still prettier than any old magazine and John said, "I think so too, Mom," and I knew they were both lying but I didn't press my luck and made both their beds for two or three weeks without complaining.

I still felt obligated to spur them on to independence. I thought a part-time job was essential as soon as they became old enough to spend money at random. Especially during their summer vacations. "Look," I told the older children, "There is no reason why you need spend the day swimming, sunbathing, and sleeping. You are healthy, young semiadults. If you want to eat and stay healthy young semiadults, perhaps you should start a summer self-supporting program. In other words—get a job!"

The only one showing any interest was seven-year-old Claudia. "I'll go to work, Mommy," she said, gathering her crayons and coloring books together. "I'll help Daddy buy groceries."

I started the campaign with David when he was sixteen. "Son," I told him, as I stood over his bed at 9:30 a.m. trying to shake him awake. "You're not going to get anywhere in life sleeping all day."

"I'm getting up," he said.

"I will tell you this," I continued at 10:30 a.m. "You'll open your eyes someday and find the world has passed you by."

"I'm getting up," he said.

At noon I pulled the sheet out from under him and shouted "Dad said if you plan to put your feet under the table this evening, you had better look for a job this afternoon—and we're having pork chops for supper." I didn't think he'd pass up a chance at pork chops. He never had.

He got out of bed, put on his clothes and complained that all the good jobs were gone. "I don't think there's a job left in this town," he said looking at a sleep-swollen face in the mirror. Wrong, I told him. True, the banks had their presidencies pretty well sewed up but I certainly didn't think there was anything disgraceful about starting at the bottom.

"When should I start looking?" he asked.

"How about today."

"It's pretty hot," he said, settling down in front of the air conditioner and the television. "I read somewhere that prospective employers frown on applicants who sweat."

"Risk it," I commanded, and turned off both the air conditioner and the television. This upset Augie-Doggie, and he growled a little and shuffled out the door. "Watch it, dog," I said. "There's nothing that says a dog can't work for a living. Dog food costs money, too, you know."

David muttered something about child labor laws and took off down the road. Later that afternoon I noticed that he wheeled into the yard with a certain flair. I noticed that probably for the first time in the bike's life it was placed carefully in an upright position on its kickstand instead of being tossed down in my geraniums. I noticed, too, that he looked three inches taller and a couple of years older.

"Hi, Mom!" he called out. Was I mistaken . . . had his voice completely changed in a few hours? "Have you started those pork chops yet?"

"No," I answered, "not yet."

"Well, don't," he said proudly. "I got a job. I'm taking you and Dad out for supper. We'll have pizza. And I'm paying." Another grownup in the family.

And as the children grew up I determinedly recorded their growth with a camera. I suppose in a period of about twenty years I spent enough money on snapshots to purchase a lakeside home, a mink stole, and our own private Silver Jet. I have no snapshots of our children's first steps, first haircuts, or first dates, but I have albums full of the first grasshopper of the season, the first cobweb of the year, and the hole in the screen door as it opened on Karen's first escort.

"What is it?" Lee asked the day I proudly showed him a pair of blurred legs running out of the corner of the photograph. It was obvious to me. I thought anyone could see it. It was a permanent record of a great family event. It was either (1) David catching a frisbee, (2) Mary chasing a butterfly, or (3) one of the children running away from home.

"You don't focus," Lee complained. "All of your pictures are fuzzy." He was just bad-mouthing because the shot I took of him with his first (and only) Canadian goose looked as if he was holding a shimmering white ghost by the foot. And you really couldn't tell it was a goose. In fact, unless you knew him intimately, you couldn't even tell it was him. Unfortunately, I cooked the goose before I could get another picture.

"Not all my pictures are fuzzy," I said, and proudly proved this by producing several clear, sharp snapshots of the vacant lot across from our house. Each weed stood out with incredible flawlessness.

Could there be a tiny little man inside my camera, sitting there, deliberately screwing up the pictures I wanted to take? "I'll just take care of this one," he must have sneered to himself as I posed a succession of toddlers with Augie-Doggie. It was an ideal set-up. The rehearsed masterpiece of small child plus cute dog. The toddler offers the cute big dog a bone. Big dog looks sweetly at the child, a smile flickering across his gentle mouth. A fluffy cloud sails across the background and brightly-colored bachelor buttons dip in the breeze, encircling the entire scene with vivid brilliance. This was one time I was convinced I had taken the perfect picture. I even used colored film. The picture developed in black and white. The only real color was on a red thumb print covering the toddler's face. Augie-Doggie was a gray rock. He had no features, and you couldn't tell it was a cute, big dog. It looked like an ugly, big lump with a tail. Not only had the toddler lost his face but he had lost his diaper, and the white cloud had been replaced by a dust storm which botched up the background, and the bachelor buttons had disappeared altogether. Actually, it was one of my better efforts, and I thought about having it framed.

When we looked at vacation pictures I had taken we couldn't tell Canada from Kansas. "What's that?" Lee squinted, trying to decide if it was a mountain or a prairie-dog town.

"That's Minnesota!" Claudia said in triumph. "Look, there's the top of a lake right there in the middle."

"No, it isn't," John argued. "It's Wyoming. I see the shadows of the oil well."

"It can't be Wyoming," I told him. "None of our Wyoming pictures turned out except the one of Daddy coming out of the wooden outhouse. Remember?"

"I remember," John grinned. It remains the best picture

137

I have ever taken. I had it blown up and gave it to Auntie-dear for Christmas.

"I bet it's Arkansas," I said, after studying the sky with concentration. "I can nearly make out the tail of that twister we were caught in."

"It isn't Arkansas, Mom," I was quickly told. "You were so scared of the storm you left the camera in that ditch you made us all lay down in and Daddy wouldn't go back for it and you cried and we didn't get any supper that night because everyone was mad. Besides, it wasn't a twister. It was just a simple rain storm. It didn't even thunder."

"You remember your way, I'll remember mine," I said, and knew that some day in a real emergency they would thank me for my alert reactions just as some day they would appreciate my photographic efforts and be glad they had a mother who spent sixty dollars a week on film and processing instead of food. Some day, when they were all very old and attending a family reunion, they would gather around the fat albums, turning the pages, and say to one another in intimate reminiscence . . .

"Who is that, for God's sake!" I just know they will.

21

Please God, Can I Wear Jeans in Heaven?

When Karen's kindergarten teacher sent home a list of telephone numbers and suggested we help her practice calling her friends, I thought that teacher must be the world's cleverest woman. Lee warned me there might be a problem or two connected to this new accomplishment. "How can you think that?" I asked him. "Look, she has done nothing more constructive with her life than dress dollies. Now she can call friends on the telephone. That is an achievement. Something she can use the rest of her life. Our little girl is growing up."

"You're right," he answered, "and there is little doubt that she will grow up thinking God pays the telephone bills."

"Doesn't He?" I tucked my eyes down shyly, hoping the comparison would mellow him. It didn't.

"Mark my words," he said, "you'll live to regret this, and I wash my hands of the whole affair. Don't come to me complaining about the insane teacher who instructs little children in the use of the telephone. Just don't come to me when you can no longer get near it."

But of course I did. There was no one else to turn to. The other children had no sympathy, and Augie couldn't care less. When I tried to confide in the mailman, he flipped my flag down and drove away. I would've told my best friend, but she had a daughter the same age and we could never call each other on the telephone. Once in a while we ran into each other at the grocery store and talked about the long-lost days when we could remember each other's telephone numbers. But it wasn't the same. Nothing was. I don't think I've had a personal telephone call in about fifteen years, but I can definitely remember what it was like and how it used to be. Oh yes, I can remember the excitement I felt when the telephone rang and I was sure it was for me. My heart skipped a beat, the adrenalin pumped, and my mouth went dry. Springing from my chair, I raced across the room in anticipation. Was it a call telling me I had won the *Reader's Digest* sweepstakes? Was it a TV quiz show offering me a thousand dollars? Was it Robert Redford? It never was, but in my heart I thought it might be. I never gave up hope. It was breathtaking . . . stimulating . . . it was life's drama at its highest. Now I sit here, all hope gone from my future. Lee tried hard not to say "I told you so," and I turned into an answering service.

"Hello!" I said into the telephone cheerfully. As cheerfully as I can to someone who doesn't want to talk to me, that is. "No, she isn't home, but I bought new curtains for the kitchen. No, I don't know when she is coming home, but I'd be glad to give you the recipe for my famous stuffing that you can eat like pizza. Yes, I will tell her you called, and by the way, did you know the Smiths are having marital problems? And yes," I sigh, "I suppose she is going to the game and will meet you there and isn't this weather awful and I heard the stores downtown are having a big sale tomorrow and why are you hanging up without even saying good-bye?" Rude, rude.

Lee claimed our girl-babies were born with a dial tone and their forefingers curved. "I'm sure," he told anyone who would listen, "when they get to heaven they will be the only angels whose wing tips give off busy signals." Perhaps he is right. Perhaps they do talk in area code and I'm the only one who understands them, but he's under the impression that you need only use the telephone for birth, marriage, and death, and even then you limit the call to three minutes. Anything said beyond that time limit, he says, is insignificant.

I found raising a teen-aged Karen a unique adventure. One that I wouldn't have traded for all the football players in the world. And it didn't matter a whit whether I had one daughter, three daughters, or five . . . each was an experience. Especially when I took them shopping in a department store or tried to give them advice about boys.

At one stage my name meant "Magic." Who else could produce an authentic witch's costume for Halloween in thirty minutes, or sneak a stitch in a junior high home ec project without the teacher knowing, or make seventeen dozen cookies for a Brownie meeting and not break the Brownie promise by swearing, and who else but a mother could admit that I, too, lost when I tried out for cheerleader but managed to survive . . . and marry . . . after all.

Karen often felt better just knowing I was in the kitchen. But when she entered senior high school, she forgot to admit it. Suddenly that magic was gone. It was no longer there—at least, not so anyone could see it. I did the best I could, but it definitely wasn't enough.

My sewing machine, still holding bobbin thread from the last witch's suit, stood idle. How could I sew for someone who was never home and who wouldn't have worn it even if she had been? Never mind that she had picked it out the material and the pattern herself and had promised faithfully that she definitely was interested in the economics of home sewing and said how lucky she was to have a handy mother. Somehow, good old handy mother took a tuck in the wrong place and threw the whole grain off and it didn't look like the garment in the picture and no one . . . absolutely no one . . . wore homemade clothes anyway.

In a period of six months I had become mentally deficient, terribly clumsy, and absolutely impossible. Karen couldn't, for the life of her, understand how her father had managed to fall in love with such a lady, and sometimes I had trouble with that one myself. The only one who seemed to be in full control was Lee. He had no problems at all. He simply continued to love us both.

I often had to look back in the family album to reassure myself that I was dealing with the right person. Where once her room had been full of Barbie doll clothes and music boxes, suddenly it was a habitat for gross posters and eight-track tape decks. She was seldom seen without a telephone in one hand and a blow dryer in the other. Washing her hair replaced going to the zoo. Her security blanket was a bottle of shampoo, and she no longer ended her nightly prayer with "God Bless Mommy and Daddy" but with "Please, God, can I wear jeans in heaven?"

And then all at once . . . one by one . . . in a blink of an eye . . . our daughters started to go. Perhaps they went to college, to a job, an apartment or dorm, or married and had their own homes. Maybe they were in Colorado, Chicago, or California, or only down the street or across town, but the important thing, the lonesome thing was they were no longer home.

The house no longer smelled of an overdose of cheap cologne, and something could be served for supper besides potato chips. My makeup box remained intact and my mascara hadn't been to a basketball game in months. My pantyhose no longer rock-and-rolled out the door and Lawrence Welk could blow his champagne bubbles in peace, without fear of being quickly erased by the flick of a switch. There wasn't one wispy bra in the wash and the bathtub was alarmingly clean.

Peace had come to the Lueth household, but it wasn't the same. Something was definitely missing, and I was the first to notice. It was strange. Life wasn't as much fun as it used to be. And then came a call or a letter or a drop-in visit from a grown-up daughter. She needed her *mother's* advice. Mother, the mentally deficient one. She actually wanted to ask me a question.

"Mother," she said, "it's that witch's costume I'm making for your granddaughter. She says the hat isn't pointed right. She says she won't wear it until it looks just so. How in the world did you do it? How did you ever make me into such a perfect witch?"

It was easy, I told her. I had a perfect daughter.

22

Who Says
Mothers Can't Cry a Little

Soaring over blooming lilacs, fresh spring raindrops, nodding tulips, bird nests important with new life, misty mornings, and warm breezes, an important person who couldn't
be overlooked stepped out into the world—our high school
graduate.

One by one they stepped over the threshold, leaving the
days of weekly allowances, parent-signed permission slips,
teacher-signed hall passes, being grounded, getting after-
school detentions, monitored bathrooms, curfew, hot lunch
programs, band practice, and living through the day after
a best friend was elected prom queen or football king and
they weren't.

Their dad and I welcomed them to the other world.
Suddenly, the parental money tree was to take root worm
and die. It was time for them to take up an exciting full-
time job to earn money for college, marriage, or a new
car—whichever was to come first—and to eat. Their dad
advised them that unfortunately they couldn't go to college, get married, buy a new car, and eat all at the same
time. This was where the grown-up fun came in. They had
to make some of their own decisions, he told them, even if
they were wrong, and once in a while, in a real emergency,
they could call on us.

For our graduates it was the excitement of packing
brand new luggage full of jeans and T-shirts, leaving home
for the first time, and coming back to find a little sister
had moved into their bedroom without even asking. They
found out that laundromats were quarter eaters and that

143

bleach drilled holes in their good underwear if they threw too much in at once, and they wondered why they hadn't realized their dad was on an intellectual plane high above everyone else even when he was dozing off in front of the television, and that I hadn't screamed and ranted and raved just to entertain the neighbors.

They found out, and admitted, that they missed Augie-Doggie greeting them with a lick and a wag when they came home to a sleeping house late at night and that our house smelled different from anyone else's, and that somehow the other smells in strange places were never quite right. And their minds wandered to what was going on along about 7:30 p.m. when they were a little bit lonely and they knew things at home were safe and serene. And they found out that no one took the blame for their actions but themselves and when they cried, no one really cared.

Lee and I watched hundreds and hundreds of teen-agers in identical caps and gowns marching to the strains of "Pomp and Circumstance" and saw only one! And we bought new luggage for the graduate, knowing full well what it signified and understanding that when each of them shouted, "I can't wait to leave home!" they really didn't mean it. And when they were finally gone, we ran down that automatic child check-list at 10 p.m. and wondered what they were doing, realizing we didn't know and praying they did. We kind of wished that old money tree could take root and make it easy and right for them, but knew it wouldn't benefit them if it did.

As parents, Lee and I hoped there were kind, gentle people out there where they were going, knowing full well there weren't and wanting to warn them to stay away from those who weren't and knowing full well they wouldn't. And we hoped that new roommates or husbands or wives could be tolerant of the fact they were sometimes careless with sunflower seeds and candy bar wrappers and that they didn't always pick up after themselves in the bathroom or make their bed and that sometimes they lost toothbrushes, razors, important papers, their tempers, and common sense, and we hoped they would help them find these things like we had done over the years.

It was not easy for me to sit quietly through a graduation ceremony. Instinct made me feel obligated to temporarily squash any enthusiasm for independent living that might be lurking in the printed words of a diploma handed to my child by a perfect stranger. What right did he have to shake their hands, smile, and say, "Go now, into the world, it is yours!" They were mine. And I wasn't sure I wanted them to go.

We counted the freckles and the memories as each of our high school graduates stepped proudly down the aisle with their classmates.

Where does it say in a parents' handbook that a mother can't cry a little?

IF GOD HAD WANTED THEM TO GO TO COLLEGE, HE WOULD HAVE PAID THEIR TUITION

College-Age Stage

23

College is a Big Step

I felt the least John could have done when he went off to college was pause long enough to say good-bye instead of zipping out the door with a casual "See you." I didn't expect him to weep and wail and throw his body across the threshold, hanging onto the screendoor, but he could've hesitated a little. He just held out his hand for tuition money and left. A friend told me she woke up every night with big knots in her stomach when her first child went to college. I knew how she felt. I had heard stories about college life, too. What neither of us realized at the time was the fact most of those stories were true. I wondered how her stomach would react when she found that out.

I couldn't understand why he went off with such a big grin on his face. Why, I remembered when he hesitated to go to the summer shows because he hated to leave his mother's side, and that wasn't so long ago. "College is a big step," I told him. "You don't swing into it with a banana Bic in one hand and a popcorn popper in the other. You have to prepare."

"I'm only going eighty miles away," he said quietly and eagerly. "It isn't like I'm going clear across the country. I'll be home often and you'll be coming down to see me . . . won't you?" For a second he wavered, but only for a second. "I can't wait for you to see my dorm room. My roommate is an only child and he is bringing a television set, a stereo, a telephone, and a refrigerator."

"Why on earth do you need a refrigerator? Your meals are furnished. We're paying for them." John said he wasn't sure, but his roommate was a sophomore and said a refrigerator was as important to college life as attending classes. John's dad hinted that he certainly hoped he had a job lined up to support the refrigerator in the manner to which refrigerators are accustomed.

Two weeks before it was time for John to leave I harbored secret thoughts that it would've been nice to have lived in a day and age when it was considered unusual to send children to college. Pioneer mothers didn't have to suffer these nerve pangs. They expected sensible things from their sons like milking cows, plowing fields, cleaning the outhouse, killing rattlesnakes, and fighting off Indians. How nice it must have been to be a mother in the olden days.

I wanted to take him down to the local men's store and outfit him in attractive slacks, handsome shirts, fashionable ties, a silk scarf, toiletries, and butter-soft leather shoes. I wanted him ready for college if it took every cent of my grocery money for the next twenty years. We could eat macaroni and cheese for months, but he would do us proud on campus. He turned down that idea and took a laundry bag stuffed full of jeans and army shirts, a personalized beer mug, and felt he was prepared to weather any scholastic or social storm. And the night before he left he took one last look at familiar furniture, his chair at the table, and his brother and sisters, gave Augie a loving shove off his foot, and announced in a proud, grown-up voice, "This is the last night I will sleep in this house as a civilian."

Was he going off to combat? I wondered. And then I worried more.

I expected him home the next weekend. He didn't come. I told Lee I didn't think he had gone to college to learn anything, anyway. "I know he's gone down there so he can live just as he pleases, surrounded by dirty clothes and paper wads." I had warned him before he left that he should keep his room tidy and nice so he could spend his time studying instead of looking in the lumps for a place to sleep.

Lee remained nonchalant about the whole affair. "He isn't going to the university to learn to be Betty Crocker. He's majoring in business."

"But what will his housemother think?" I said, choking up.

"What housemother!" Lee snickered.

Well, that's when I insisted we run down to see how he was getting along. I didn't care if he had been gone only ten days. No housemother, indeed. Who in the world would be responsible for seeing that he got in by ten o'clock on school nights and that he wore pajamas to bed, brushed his teeth in the morning, changed his underwear, and would screen the girls he dated to see that they were from nice families? Lee laughed out loud at that, but promised to drive me down there to see him. I called Karen, who was married by now, to tell her where we'd be in case she wondered, asked Susan, who worked and lived in her own apartment, to come supervise at home, fixed up a box of cookies, carrots, chunky cheese, and cleanser, and started to pack an overnight bag.

"Why in the world are you taking your nightgown?" Lee asked. "We are only going to be there a couple of hours. We aren't sleeping in."

"But what if he wants me to stay overnight?"

"He won't. Believe me, he won't."

I left the suitcase at home and took my heartiest and healthiest philodendron named Phyllis instead.

"Why are you taking a plant?"

"To keep him company and give him someone to talk with." Unfortunately poor Phyllis met an untimely death a few weeks after she entered college. John's roommate arose in the middle of the night to answer a call of nature and answered it on poor Phyllis. She died a sudden and I suppose horrible death.

I imagined terrible things on our trip to the university. I was positive John had probably lost forty-five pounds, his hair, and most of his teeth from the lack of good home cooking. I visualized his clothing in shreds and him in tears as he cried himself to sleep every night. Probably his roommate was a ghoul and a bad influence, and I decided right then and there that I would have a chat with the university chancellor about the type of student he allowed to attend a state university. After all, we paid taxes to support it, didn't we? I would think I would have

151

some say so about the way things were run. Lee didn't think so.

When we drove into the city limits of the town housing the university, its bright seamy lights blinded me. Every corner and every storefront screamed wickedness. I was positive taverns and tarts lay in wait for unsuspecting college freshmen. Lee told me not to be silly. He told me it was still the same city we had shopped in only six weeks before. "It hasn't changed," he said. "You even told me it would be a nice place to be buried in because it has such a peaceful, dignified aura about it."

"I've changed my mind," I said firmly.

We stopped and asked directions to the dormitory from a girl carrying books and crossing the street. A girl with slothful eyes and lustful hips. To me, she looked far too old to be attending college. I was sure the books were only a front. With a gesture exclusively reserved for experienced ladies-of-the-night, she slung back her long blonde hair (it needed washing), slithered sensuously toward the car, lowering her knees and gazing into Lee's face, and said, "Oh, you mean The Zoo . . . it's that way." She pointed toward the tallest of four or five dormitories.

"Did you see that!" I gasped, clutching Lee's arm. "If that's the caliber of girl John is thrown in with every day, boy, we're just going to take him back home with us."

"She seemed like a perfectly nice girl to me," Lee said. "Wholesome as apple pie. I bet she's a cheerleader."

Four hundred stereos blared four hundred different loud rock songs as we entered the dorm, and I didn't see any padlocked steel doors separating the boys' part from the girls' part. I put that at the top of my Chancellor List. Other parents were wandering through the corridors with frightened, puzzled, lost looks on their faces. It was as if, at middle-age, we had been plunged into a youthful hell.

"How in the world do you ever study in all this noise and confusion?" I asked John as the three of us stood in the middle of his room admiring his refrigerator. "I don't see how you can possibly study." John smiled secretly as he eyed . . . definitely eyed . . . three slender, very seductive young freshmen girls as they wiggled past his open door. I don't think studying was uppermost in his mind. I think he was going to leave the studying worry up to Mother and Dad. I think he had other things to worry about. At this point, so did my stomach and I.

"Well, Mother, how do you think he looks?" Lee said, clapping John on the back with a hearty he-man swat. I had to admit he looked pretty good. I think he had gained weight, his hair looked fluffy, his teeth were clean and all firmly in place, his clothes were rumpled but washed, and the brief appearance of his roommate proved him to be perfectly acceptable. John said the food was great, everyone was friendly, the instructors helpful, and he loved college and intended to stay there for the rest of his life. (He nearly did, too.)

"Now, remember," I told him as he bent down to hug me good-bye. "You really don't have to stay here if you don't want to. You can come home. I'm sure I can find some rattlesnakes for you to kill and Indians for you to fight." He looked at me with a puzzled look. "You'll be all right, Mom, as soon as you get some fresh air. I'll write," he promised.

When Lee and I stepped out into the cool outside, the sound of heavy traffic, squealing brakes, whistles, and diesel engines was like the hum of a lazy bee in comparison to the inside of the dormitory. We were safe. But was he?

Of course he was. And as each of our other children marched off to college life, my reactions slowed down as did my suspicions of refrigerators in their rooms, noise in the hallways, and strange smoky smells in the elevators. I accepted their collect calls, urgent pleas for more money, dirty laundry, and the fact I was going to be forced to fight my own Indians and kill my own damn rattlesnakes all by myself.

But that didn't mean I was going to have to like it.

24

Won't Someone
Please Take Charlie?

Toward the end of my child-bearing years I began to have serious doubts about our family planning skills. For some reason, when each child was born we didn't think about college education, and it was something of a surprise to us when suddenly John, David, and Mary were all attending the same university at the same time. Again I thought of approaching the chancellor, this time for special rates. "We deserve them, I think," I told Lee.

"I don't think he'll listen."

"But don't you suppose we could get ten percent off for bulk?"

"It doesn't work that way," Lee said impatiently. "For one thing, the university doesn't give discounts, and for another they figure your sex life is your business and if you have one child or a dozen it's of no interest to them."

"Well, I don't know about this college business anyway," I said vehemently. "They don't have parent-teacher conferences, or get-acquainted teas for the parents so we can meet the instructors and see the classrooms."

"It's not high school. Many college students are considered consenting adults."

"That sounds awful. I hope Mary doesn't go around consenting."

"I don't mean that type of consenting. I mean they are able to make their own decisions."

"Without their mother?"

"Without their mother!" Lee said stubbornly, ending the

154

conversation by leaving the house and going to the garage to saw things.

I had no intentions of giving up that easily. That university wasn't going to snatch my children. I tried sending little bits of home with each of them to remind them of their roots. I sent John a hanging begonia to replace poor dead Phyllis. With Dave I sent two giant and quite homely cacti which he called Sticky and Sam. I gave Mary a rubber plant named America. It was magnificent, with shiny fat leaves, and it thrived on college life. So did Mary. She had taken John's place in The Zoo and both he and David lived off-campus in separate apartments. But I couldn't get any of them to take Charlie, no matter how hard I tried.

Charlie was our House Ghost, and as each of our children left home and went to college I tried sending him along. I even offered to pay his tuition. I felt he could use the education, and I certainly needed a vacation from him. He had been with us for years, haunting our house, and I wanted to get rid of him, if only for a semester or two. I had realized our house was infested with a spooky presence when I discovered, day after day, dirty dishes in the living room and empty ice-cube trays in the refrigerator. I knew it wasn't me who had finished off the vodka in the liquor cabinet or scattered newspapers all over the house, and if I could believe the rest of the members of our family, they hadn't done it either. There was no one left but Charlie.

"Who's Charlie?" David had asked the first time he heard me say, "Darn that Charlie, he's at it again." Down deep he didn't really care who Charlie was; he was most happy that, for once, he wasn't getting all the blame.

"He's our ghost," I answered, lowering my voice in order to create the right effect. "Every good house has a ghost." Claudia began to cry and I had to quickly explain that Charlie was a good ghost, a friendly ghost, much like Casper. I reassured her that Charlie wouldn't swoop down from our ceiling and carry her off to his crypt even if her brothers had told her he would. I explained that Charlie was nice, not naughty.

Eventually, the whole family accepted Charlie. Even Lee with his orderly, statistical, no-nonsense mind. "You know, of course, that I don't believe in ghosts," he said, but in the next breath he asked, "Why Charlie? Why not Charlene?" I told him that was simple enough. Our ghost had to be male. No lady ghost went around letting the lid on the bathroom stool remain up, leaving herself wide open to a plunge into the depths at 3 a.m. Lee and the boys insisted they carefully replaced everything they used in our bathroom to its original state. Why, then, did I find myself sinking into oblivion and gripping cold edges in terror and shock when I forgot to turn the lights on at night? It certainly wasn't Charlene.

Augie-Doggie was probably the last to be convinced, but after sauntering up to his dog dish some million times and finding it empty, he became resigned, sat back on his haunches, rolled his eyes heavenward, and dog-muttered, "Stupid ghost, I hope you choke!" He knew good and well I had not eaten his food, he hadn't, and since everyone swore they fed him just as I ordered, it only left Charlie.

Charlie was the one who poked holes in the screen door to let homeless flies and mosquitos find shelter inside our house. He was the one who erased important telephone messages that certain people vowed they had written down carefully. He tossed gum wrappers in the ashtrays, shoes in the halls, banana peels on the front porch, several brands of beer cans in the garbage—and he had to be the one who put his supernatural foot through my brand new Austrian pouf panel curtains in our bedroom, ripping out four poufs, just like that. Lee swore he didn't do it, even though I had heard him, only an hour before, mumbling something about my putting lace on his pajamas next. He said just because he hated those curtains, it didn't mean he'd deliberately tear them up. He said he supposed it was that silly ghost. Well, all I can say is Charlie needed his mouth washed out with soap. I heard what he said when those curtains were shredding. I heard him clear down in the kitchen.

Charlie was always the first one up in the morning. He had to be the one who crept downstairs and ate all the sugar-coated cereal in the house, leaving the empty box sitting beside Amy's bed. She said she knew all along this was everyone's favorite and the last box in the house and she wouldn't do such a thing. And he must have been the one who dashed about pushing in alarm clock buttons so that no one would get up in the morning. Everyone claimed they would've popped right out if Charlie hadn't been monkeying around. After all, they said, we can't react to an alarm if we don't hear it. It really stimulated good old Charlie when he heard me trying to get everyone up in the morning and off to school. They were very hard to get out of bed under normal circumstances, but with Charlie's fine hand showing, they were impossible. I could almost hear him giggling when I had a late afternoon fit early in the morning.

He followed me all day long. He put the cheese cutter in the garbage can, unrolled the toilet paper, burned the bottom of my best frying pan, unraveled all my white thread, chewed holes in the vacuum cleaner bags, and sat on the television antenna, jiggling it and hopping off only when the repair man came, making the picture as clear as a bell by convincing the television man I was nuts and out to molest him.

Zapping a cobweb in a prominent corner of the living room, he tilted the lamp like a spotlight so Mr. Spider could be on center stage, and he turned a perfectly adjusted house pet into a neurotic lap dog . . . a BIG, neurotic lap dog. It wouldn't have been so bad if Augie had chosen my lap or Lee's lap, but he always picked the lap of Auntie-dear, who was not only allergic to but deathly afraid of dogs. We always removed the dog quickly, but not before Auntie-dear had turned limp and had dog hair all over her. You could almost visualize Charlie clapping his hands and turning somersaults. Lee liked Charlie a lot when Auntie-dear came to visit, he said.

But occasionally I needed good old Charlie to fall back on when nothing else seemed to work. And sometimes I needed him worse than other times. I was especially grateful that his phantom presence solved the mystery of the disjointed pipe. For a while there, Lee was trying to blame the whole incident on me.

The garbage disposal stopped up and I was prepared to take the blame for that. I could hardly push it off on an innocent ghost when the entire family had watched me peel the potatoes for dinner and shove too many scraps down the disposal. Lee was ready to go play golf when the garbage disposal started spitting up. He was dressed in a new knit shirt, clean white trousers, and he looked very nice.

"It will only take a minute to fix it." I told him. "All you have to do is go into the cellar and jiggle a few things. You jiggle so well, I wouldn't think of doing it myself." Besides, I didn't go into that cellar. There were stranger things than ghosts down there.

Painfully, Lee descended the stairs and I could hear him tinkering and toying with pipes and things and I was secure in the knowledge that the disposal would soon be chewing and chucking stuff again. Lee is very good about fixing things. I busied myself in the kitchen, puttering with mundane chores and singing country western songs. I simply forgot that the disposal didn't work, that Lee was in the cellar, and that he was dressed and clean and kind. I flipped its switch and waited.

A giant roar filled the kitchen and Lee entered from the bowels of the earth, his neat knit shirt and the top of his neat head covered with tiny bits and pieces of potato peel, orange rind, and lettuce leaves.

"Who was the idiot who turned on the garbage disposal while I had the pipe disconnected?" he screamed. "Screamed" is the word. I can't think of a better one.

I wanted to dissolve, but I couldn't. I had to face his wrath and come up with something fantastic or face the possibility of being carefully placed, head down, in the garbage disposal. So I lied.

"It was Charlie-the-ghost," I said with every ounce of persuasiveness I had in my body, "that darned Charlie-the-ghost. It had to be him. I wouldn't do that. You know I wouldn't do a thing like that on purpose." Oh, believe me, I prayed silently.

I don't think he really did believe me, but he let me get by with it. It had something to do with true love and acceptance of his fate.

"Thank you, Charlie," I said quietly to the sink. And I really think I heard a ghostly gurgle from the depths of the disposal. And, so, Charlie is still with me. He didn't go to college and there are times when I am quite glad he didn't.

25

Pitch It or Wash It

With the two older girls out on their own, three in college, and Amy and Claudia left at home, our entire life style took on a different slant.

"I'm going to become a good housekeeper now that I have more time," I said proudly to Lee. He smiled, lowered his eyes, and swallowed his comeback. He nearly choked. "There's really no excuse now for me not to keep the house neat and clean. Of course, I'll need your co-operation."

"I knew you would," he said.

I began by throwing away newspapers, and this hurt. I was a compulsive keeper of newspapers. I hoarded them as some women hoarded recipes. There was no real reason for it. Possibly it was because I knew how much hard work went into them. I could never have lived with my conscience if I lined a bird cage with newspapers. I'd use bed sheets first, and that could be one of the reasons why we never did own a bird.

I won't say that I threw away with abandon, but I did toss a lot. After two weeks of concentrated effort I counted 1500 things that I needed desperately and had to replace. Lee and the girls became paranoid. They were afraid to undress for bed.

"If she doesn't pitch it, she washes it," Amy complained. "I can't find my homework or my underwear."

"Did you look in the washer?" Claudia asked.

"I did, and my complete geometry assignment was wiped out in one rinse, but my bra had three theorems and two planes outlined on the straps. My teacher didn't believe me, and there was no way I could prove I had my assignment without doing a strip tease in class." I didn't believe her, either.

Lee started sorting through the garbage cans out by the curb before he came into the house at night, and I told him the neighbors would think he was strange if he kept that up. He said it was worth anything anyone thought if he could rescue his good sabre saw or the bill from our insurance company. "If the insurance lapses because of nonpayment, it might not matter if you keep the house clean or not." I promised him I would be more careful in the future, if he would stop looking through the garbage or at least wait until after dark when no one could see him.

He suggested that since I was throwing things away I should probably do something about my dress form . . . good old Sally Stitch. He looked longingly toward his treasure trove of garbage cans.

"Don't anyone touch my dress form," I screamed, putting my arms protectively around her headless body. "I need her."

"Why do you need it? The only time I've seen you use it in months was to drip-dry that awful afghan Auntie-dear sent us last Christmas. Do you know how scary that thing is at night when you run into it?"

"That's not very nice," I pouted. "You know it is supposed to be molded to my exact measurements. You know that is supposed to be *me*. Is that how you feel when you run into me in the dark?"

"Don't be silly," he said, patting my hip. "You're soft. She's wiry. I can tell the difference."

I suppose my dress form wasn't particularly attractive. It was lumpy, proportion-wise, but then, so am I, and it wobbled a little and it really did look more appealing when covered with an afghan, ugly or not. But over the years, good old Sally Stitch had become a familiar and true friend. She stood near my sewing machine like a large wire soldier, guarding needles and thread without taking a break. I could talk to her when I was lonely and bored with patching, or vent my frustration on her when pointed collars turned out round as I was sewing. She didn't talk back, play loud music, take my scissors, quarrel over trivia, bark, smoke smelly cigars, snore, throw her socks behind the big chair, put candy wrappers in the flower pots, or complain about my tunafish casseroles.

I have to admit she was awkward as hell to move about, for she was somewhat delicate. One false punch in the wrong spot and her shape shifted. One day during a fit of cleaning I made the mistake of asking our local Maytag man to help me move her while he was there to fix the washing machine. My arms were full of solutions and rags and he wasn't doing anything, anyway, but lying on his stomach peering into the insides of my washer. His eyes dilated with apprehension and I thought he was going to bolt from the house without being paid.

"How do you carry her?" he said rolling his eyes until only the whites showed, his hands trembling. "Where do I put my fingers?"

"Just pick her up and move her," I said. "Don't be timid. You won't hurt her. She's a tough old bird."

"What if I drop her?" he said nervously, plucking at his clothing. Possibly he had Sally Stitch mixed up with an African voodoo doll, and thought by dropping her I might break a rib. I assured him the worst possible thing that could happen was that her hips would end up where her shoulders were, and vice versa.

That silly man took twenty minutes moving that dress dummy, and charged us time and a half, while Augie barked and chased his tail for fifteen minutes because he was so excited.

In keeping with my new image, I trained myself to place a centerpiece in the middle of the kitchen table every day. I had admired this trait in others and felt it showed exceptional class. I didn't always get the toast crumbs and egg whites off the table top in the process, but as I explained to Lee when he pointed this out, we can't expect perfection. The centerpiece did have a few drawbacks, I discovered. Each time we sat down to eat, it blocked our view of the food and of one another, and if I moved it too often, the silk flowers faded and drooped. Its greenery soon became tipped with brown coffee stains, and I set it on fire twice with my cigarette. Lee heaved it out the door when his tie got caught in a sprig, and the cat ate two of the artificial elves perched on the yellow daisy. Finally I put it away until I could search the shops for one that could be wound up and walked about, and would stay out of the way on its own. I only brought it out for special company.

It was the same with the bath towels. I couldn't imagine anyone but a royal family having a constant supply of plush, thick bath towels that matched hanging permanently in their bathrooms. Evidently there were no royal children with dirty hands.

For some reason our towels continued to turn spindly and frayed and sopping wet the minute I took them from the store's sack. And they turned ugly colors. I would say that we probably owned six hundred wafer-thin grimy green bath towels. In desperation I bought fat thirsty ones, two of each, that I could pair up graciously. The fabric and shade were the best and most expensive I could get, and they balanced perfectly with the decor of our bathroom. I threatened Lee and the girls—"Never, never, let me see you using the good towels, with or without permission. Stick to the grimy green ones." I was like a black widow spider in her web. I scurried and skittered quickly through the house, hanging fine towels and dragging out the centerpiece when the doorbell rang, and removing them the minute a guest left the house. But I had to move fast. If I didn't, someone immediately used the soft, luxurious, very costly terry cloth towels to sponge down Augie, wipe up the shower, or drop on the bedroom floor. If I hadn't put away the centerpiece, they probably would have done the same with that.

I caught Claudia coming from the shower with her freshly shampooed hair wrapped in one of the good towels. Jerking it from her head, I nearly separated her neck from her shoulders. She let out a terrified yell. "OW! You're trying to kill me." No, I told her, I wasn't deliberately trying to kill her . . . just warn her.

David came home for the weekend, stood in the middle of the house, and stared. "Where are the dust balls?" he asked pitifully. "Where are the streaked windows, the stacked papers? Where are the ragged rugs, pinched pillows, and careless clothes? Where is my 'Home Sweet Home'? This is a stranger's house. My memories don't live here."

I suggested he go into the bathroom, where he'd be more

comfortable. I knew he'd recognize the towels. Later, I found him sitting on the edge of the bathtub, clutching a frazzled and shredded grimy green bath towel. He was holding it close like a security blanket. "I feel so much more comfortable in here," he explained. "This is my background. There for a while it was as if I had suddenly lost my identity."

His dad poked his head in the bathroom and told him not to worry. "The new will wear off soon, and your mother will grow tired of all this tidy stuff and things will revert to the way they were. She can't keep this pace up forever. It isn't natural. In fact, she's already started to slow down. She hasn't vacuumed the stairway in weeks."

I don't know what they expected. I had been much too busy to vacuum. I had been moving centerpieces and changing towels.

26

Enter at Your Own Risk

"How can you live this way?" I asked Mary the evening we arrived to move her from her dorm room at The Zoo to her upstairs room at home. It was spring outside, and pure and total disaster inside. She had not packed, prepared, or pushed things around. Instead, she was resting quietly on her bed, her nose brushing the ceiling. A perfectly nice, normal-sized twin bed had been elevated into a stiltlike sleeper by the boxes, bagels, books, bones, bags, bottles, balls, banners, bathing suits, baskets, baubles, and bacteria shoved beneath it. She couldn't get one more thing under that bed without going through to the sky.

"My God," Lee said, "we will never get all of this in the car," and he sat down on the closest pile of dirty stockings. His body settled in comfortably. "We only have a normal, ordinary automobile, not a semi." I could almost swear he choked back a sob. He looked defeated. This man who had efficiently fed, clothed, housed, and managed a family of nine for nearly thirty years had suddenly reached his level of incompetence when faced with moving a college daughter home for the summer holidays.

"Some of it is mine," a small voice said.

"Who's that?" I screamed, jerking around to see if some of the dirt had hatched and Mary was sharing a room with a germy spook. A closer inspection uncovered her roommate, hidden behind three stop signs and a pair of horn-rimmed glasses.

"Hello, dear," I said. "Are your folks coming tonight to help you move?" I certainly hoped so.

"Oh no." She recoiled into her sheets. "I told them not to come until you had been here. My mother would die if she saw this mess. You all go right ahead. Don't mind me. I'll just sit here and watch." Bless you, my dear, I thought, for you have a poor attitude.

I'm sure we could've furnished a six-room house with the contents of this one, very small, eight-by-ten room. Stepping gingerly through wadded tissues and crumpled posters, I made my way across the room. I hoped and prayed that I would step on nothing that squashed and grunted or reached up to grab me by the ankle. "We have to start somewhere," I said. "Let's get some boxes and plastic bags and get with it." I was tempted to open the window and start heaving, but litter laws prevented me from doing so. That and the campus police officer stationed outside the window on the sidewalk.

Mary vaulted from her bed and Lee moved a red knee sock from beneath his chin and we started sorting. Occasionally, the roommate peeked out to check on our progress.

"Oh, there's my pink blouse," she yelled triumphantly. "I've been looking for that since October." It had been resting comfortably between a granny apron I had sent along for Mary to wear while cleaning her room and the telephone number of a hit man for her to contact in case she was approached by a pervert in the elevator. Obviously, neither had been used. They looked as good as new.

Mary handed over the pink blouse and reminded her roommate that she still had her favorite hard rock album at *her* house. "You took it home for Thanksgiving, remember?"

"My mother listens to it when she cleans the oven," Mary explained. "She's always thought cleaning the oven was the most horrible thing she knew of until she heard that album. Now, she says she knows there is at least one more thing worse in this world. It keeps her going, she claims."

"Tell her she can keep the album with my compliments," I said haughtily. I pictured her mother as being one of those cleany-cleany types that crawled inside the oven to get to corners.

Searching through the debris, I uncovered several things that we had been missing at home. My good scissors popped up unexpectedly behind a gum ball. A T-shirt Amy had sworn Augie had eaten cuddled behind the bed post, and an ivy that I thought had been destroyed by grub worms trailed from beneath a wastebasket. A library book that I had been charged for when a stern librarian accused me of stealing it was perched on top of a lamp. "Wow!" Lee cried. "Here's my hygiene training manual I had when I was in the Navy. I've looked all over for it." I didn't ask why he had been looking for it, nor did I ask Mary why she had it in her room. Her roommate didn't want to give it up.

"I'll buy it from you," she offered. Lee said no and shoved it in his pocket.

Finally I called John and David. We needed their help. I told them their Dad and I were considering divorce and if they wanted any say-so in who got custody of the children they'd better get over to Mary's room right away. Had they known we wanted to use their flexible bones and strong young backs to carry the contents of Mary's room to our car, they wouldn't have come. I know that. They would've begged off by saying they had to study.

The five of us made trip after trip up and down in the elevator. Have you ever lugged fourteen patchwork quilts and tried not to sweat? My makeup melted, my hairdo frizzed, and I took off my high heels and put on my missing snuggie slippers I had found being used as bookmarks. "Don't tell anyone you are my mother!" Mary begged.

"Or mine," her roommate chimed in.

The last thing to leave the dorm room was the rubber plant, America. It had grown three feet and added seven new leaves since I had seen it last. "What are you feeding that thing?" I asked Mary.

"Food from the cafeteria," she answered. "We trade. On Fridays I give it my fish and I eat its plant food. It works out fine." It must, I thought. They both looked great.

"This is the last damn trip for this rubber plant," Lee yelled, shoving and poking it into the back seat. "I can't drive safely in a jungle. The plant is remaining in one spot until you have your very own home or your very own Mayflower moving van." I suggested we stop and have something to eat so he could calm down before driving home. We took Mary and the boys followed us. When we reached the restaurant Lee told us not to lock the doors of the car.

I nearly passed out right there in the parking lot, and Mary's mouth flew open. He *always* insisted we lock the car. In fact, he could get downright nasty about it on occasion. But this time he even left the keys in the ignition.

"Maybe someone will steal it," he explained optimistically, "and then we won't have to unpack when we get home." And that was the first and last time I ever knew him to think and sound like me.

27

Be Sure
To Keep Your Legs Crossed

I learned when college entered our lives and our check-books that a number of changes were due to take place in our lives. Some of the adjustments Lee and I took to perfectly and in stride. Others were harder to accept. I could never get used to:

The quiet.

Having our children turn into professional beggers. David's arm grew eight inches from stretching his hand out every time he saw us . . . palm up.

Unselfish mothers who bragged about scrubbing floors to send their children to college, wearing their tattered gingham with pride.

Not knowing what our children were doing . . . or with whom.

Watching Auntie-dear's face when she found out what they were doing and who they were doing it with.

Having John, who had holes in his socks and no warm mittens, spend his allotted money on time payments for a water bed.

Seeing a frightened and trembling Mary off on her first commercial airline flight. I had two excellent words of advice for her. "Don't go!" Her dad pooh-poohed this. He said it would be a good experience—a learning one.

"But I'm too fat to travel on an airplane," Mary said.

"What in the world does weight have to do with it?" Lee asked, puzzled. He was beginning to worry that she was starting to analyze things as I did. He had hoped college would eliminate this problem.

Mary worked very hard and lost nearly twenty pounds. I asked her how she managed to do this so easily. "I worried it off," she replied.

"But you are getting so thin," I told her, "that if you aren't careful, you're going to float away. You won't need an airplane to get you where you are going."

"That's the point. If I'm going to fall out of an airplane I prefer drifting to dumping. I don't want to thud when I hit the ground. If I weigh less I don't think I will fall so hard or splat when I get there." Lee sighed and said "Now, YOU are thinking like your mother. Losing weight isn't going to help one bit if you fall out of an airplane."

I told him he shouldn't tell her that, she was tense enough already and I knew how she felt. On a scale of one to ten, I rated flying thirteen. I think it is definitely overpublicized. The only thing I can see that you might save by flying is time, and what good are a few extra hours if you've dropped fifteen years from your normal life span in the process?

"If you'll keep your mouth shut about it," Lee warned, "she'll be all right. You are only going to upset her. You know how you blow things out of proportion."

So I simply told Mary to enjoy herself but to remember one thing—"If you must jump, be sure and keep your legs crossed!"

I never became seasoned to vacationing with grown-up children. I was beginning to like zoos and camping near swing sets and eating hot dogs and doing the fun little things that children do. I wasn't quite ready to participate in grown-up activities. When we had one or two babies still hanging on to my skirts, I begged off things like mountain climbing, riding the rapids, and hopping on the backs of horses for a thrilling and throbbing journey down the old trail. I had been able to beg off by telling Lee I would remain behind and show the younger children the sparkling lakes, spectacular sunsets, and the wee woodland animals. "Horseback riding will come later," I assured him, "when everyone is old enough to go." Now they were old enough to go and my words came back to haunt me. I had failed to tell him I hated horses.

"Come on," Lee said, "be a sport. Remember how you always wanted to join the entire family in adult fun."

"Can't we do something sensible," I argued, "like go to X-rated movies? I'll buy popcorn." No one wanted to see a dirty movie or eat popcorn—instead, they gathered enthusiastically at the corral for the hour-long trip up the steepest mountain I had ever seen in my life. They tried to tell me later it was only a little hillock. I know a hillock when I see one, and this was a mountain.

John chose a white stallion called Silver, David a brown, sleek-looking prince of a horse named King, Lee's horse was gently named Angel, and the girls picked Cookie, Patti-Ann, Pretty-face, Mandy, and Sweetie-pie.

"What is my horse's name?" I asked the gnarled old trail boss politely. He shuffled his cowboy boots in the dust and ignored me, leading a frothing animal from the stables. It had horrible yellow teeth and bad breath. "What is his name?" I repeated. I didn't look to see, I just assumed it was a he. It had long, strong muscular ears, hoofs resembling sledgehammers, and a tail that knocked down fence posts when it twitched.

"This is Mad Dog, ma'am," the wrangler grinned.

"Oh, my God," I moaned.

I stood and surveyed Mad Dog. Mad Dog, in turn, surveyed me. His hoofs pawed the ground and my knees buckled. His back was rippled with power and my spine quivered with fear.

"Mount up!" the cowboy shouted. The rest of my family promenaded from the corral like so many Roy Rogerses and Dale Evanses—proud, sprightly, and with great skill. Mad Dog and I remained in one spot and I was still on the ground. I preferred it that way. A giant hand spurted me into the saddle against my will. I won't go into detail as to how I got into the saddle, or what portions of my body the giant hand touched in order to get me there. I just know that with little dignity or personal integrity left I was sitting four stories in the air on top of an insane horse.

"Get!" And the giant hand slapped crazy old Mad Dog on the rump, barely missing mine. I could feel the air when it went by. Four large hoofs lurched into space and I slipped and rolled in the saddle like a milkshake and Mad Dog pounded the ground, making dents as large as

170

graves. Off in the distance, through scared eyes, I could see my family climbing with swaying ease the sleepy bridle path. One of their horses, probably dear little Angel, had stopped long enough to smell the daisies.

As for Mad Dog and me, we didn't make that bridle path and I didn't smell one daisy and neither did he. We spent the entire hour careening around the corral. The louder I screamed "whoa!" the faster he ran. I hung on in frenzied fear, knowing that eventually I would die in the dirt or be stapled to a fencepost.

The wrangler stopped him with a rope . . . around the horse's neck and my right leg. He offered me a free ride. He told me I could spend the whole afternoon riding. He told me I could pick out the horses I wanted and that I could even have Angel. He told me he would put Mad Dog out to pasture if I would only come out of the restroom.

I also never got used to the idea that I could become ill and remain in bed and not have to play "mother" to little children while partially blinded with a migraine, crippled with a bad back from too much childbearing, or bent over from skinned shins from bumping into twenty-three toy boxes. It didn't matter if I felt pale and wan when the children were small and needed supervision, or if my fingernails were tired or my knees upset or if the telephone rang and hurt my teeth. I still had to be strong and watch out for them. I didn't get a chance to be sick gracefully until all of them grew up.

One night I went to bed feeling perfectly normal. At 5 a.m. little tin soldiers were marching in my stomach. There must have been at least five million or so. By 5:30 they had rallied around the flag, sharpened their bayonets, and engaged in battle with the enemy. I was the enemy and I was losing the war.

"I am so sick," I said to Lee, pathetic in defeat.

"I'm so sorry," he said kindly. "Why don't you stay in bed? I will get my own breakfast and the kids are old enough to fend for themselves." With that he leaped out of bed in glowing health, jogged into the kitchen, plugged in the coffee pot, slapped three slices of bacon in a pan, cracked two eggs, turned on the toaster, and

171

dumped half a glass of jelly into a saucer. Do you know what the smell of that breakfast cooking did to those ten million little tin soldiers?

I used to dream of having a whole day of my very own just to spend in bed. In fact, while I was rinsing diapers and blowing noses, I planned all the things I would do. I planned a gala day among the bedclothes—watching television, reading a novel, doing a little embroidery, taking a nap or two, and having a luxurious luncheon complete with rosebud in vase and tea in china cup. I was going to genuinely wallow in plush pleasure. But I didn't plan to spend it with millions of little tin soldiers tramping in cadence up and down my rib cage. I tried television, and food commercials stirred up the entire regiment; the only books that interested me dealt with death and dying; I was too weak to hold an embroidery needle; and I couldn't face a soft-boiled egg, let alone a complete and luxurious luncheon. "You'll get the flu," I cautioned Augie when he flopped down beside me to take a nap. I tried hard not to breathe on his fur. I didn't want a sick dog on my hands. He looked at me with round eyes and slithered off the bed. Poor old dog, he didn't know I was sick—he thought all along it was going to be a fun day and we were going to share it.

One by one members of the family slipped into the bedroom to see if I was still fighting for my life. "Will you get well, Mommy?" Claudia asked when she came home from school that afternoon. She was worried, for she knew she was still partially dependent. She also knew I was the only chance she had to get the broken zipper fixed on her favorite jeans. If I checked out, so did her jeans. She stood at the foot of my bed with a large glass of chocolate milk and a cold hot dog in her hand. One look and one sniff and the drumbeat started, the cannon rumbled, and the little soldiers double-timed the path of gallant glory.

Amy slipped into the room. I didn't acknowledge her presence. I was taking one of my short naps and having a bad dream that no one attended my funeral services even though they were invited. I opened one eye and thought I was hallucinating. "The end is near," I decided as a large distorted monster stared at me, its grotesque face inches from mine. I took a brave breath, held it, and opened both eyes. The monster with the puffy cheeks and swollen eyes was me—a reflection in a magnified makeup mirror. Amy had it poised over my lips.

Gulping back half a troop of soldiers, I demanded to know what she was doing. "Seeing if you are still breathing," she said proudly. "I learned this in first aid class. You use a mirror. It's neat, don't you think?"

"What happened to taking a pulse?"

"Old-fashioned. Are you OK now, Mom? I hope so. Can I borrow your car?" And with that she was gone, swinging my car keys in an arc above her head. I ran up the pale flag of surrender.

John had come home to attend a bachelor party for a friend and he whipped into the bedroom, punched me on the arm, tripped over my bedroom slippers, and hurtled out the door. He didn't say a word, but I saw him look back once to see if the lump under the covers moved. Lee returned home from work and came straight to my bed. He didn't even stop long enough to hang up his coat. He put his cold hand, fresh from outside, on my fevered brow. "How do you feel?" he asked. "I'll make supper." Visions of chicken soup danced in my head. Soon an aroma crept under the door and into my sick room. It didn't smell like chicken soup!

"What are you making?" I called out in a faint, weak voice.

"Pizza."

Pizza! My God! The ten million little tin soldiers mustered for the final push. This was it. No doubt about it, they had seen the whites of my eyes. But I whipped those little soldiers, right down to the last tin hat. The pizza had done it. I adore pizza and no little soldier, tin or otherwise, was going to come between me and my stomach forever.

Lee sometimes seemed unconcerned about the changes going on in our household. He was still fighting panty-hose in the bathroom and yelling if someone or everyone didn't keep the litter box clean he was going to french-fry the cat. Wrapped up in supporting his family, mowing

173

the lawn, changing oil in the car, taking down storm windows, repairing small appliances, and hugging me on occasion, he made each day important and meaningful. He was startled when Karen announced she wanted to get married.

THE FAMILY TREE GROWS AND GROWS

Married Child Stage

28

Lose a Daughter— Gain a Son-in-Law

The day Karen told me she and Dave were planning to be married I said, "That's nice, dear. Did you pick up your room?"

"Next month," she commented nonchalantly, as she went by with an armload of dirty sheets. It took me a minute or two to realize the interval of one month involved marriage and not a time limit to clean a messy room. I wasn't surprised, because Dave had been hanging around the house for about two years, and we had grown to love him and look upon him as the tenth member of the family. I laughed nervously and told him he couldn't feign ignorance about what he was getting himself into by marrying into our family, for although he actually lived at home with his parents, he was spending more and more time before our television set, at our dinner table, on our couch, and in our driveway. Augie didn't even bark when he came to the front door, but wagged his tail, licked Dave's hand, threw up on Dave's foot, and sat between Karen and Dave when he thought it might be necessary. He was an integral part of their courtship and a darned good chaperone, I felt. I thought they might want him to be the best man at their wedding, but Dave said his brother's feelings would be hurt and Karen said if I wasn't going to take this whole thing seriously they might have to elope. Lee looked eager when she offered elopement, and volunteered to buy the gas.

I knew very little about planning a wedding. Mine had gone by in a haze, and besides, it had been such a long time ago I couldn't remember when I hadn't been married. Lee said he was having the same problem. He recalled having to buy a new suit and an orchid corsage, but beyond that he only remembered the blood test. Karen suggested perhaps the first thing to do would be make a list. We made at least five hundred lists, and I misplaced every one of them. The only one that kept reappearing on the spindle was "Buy boxer shorts—size 42," and that didn't have a thing to do with weddings.

All of us agreed the wedding should be small, intimate, and, at Lee's recommendation, cheap. The guest list was to be limited to relatives and close friends, and reached six thousand seven hundred and ninety in forty-five minutes. When I noticed Karen sticking pins in places like Alaska, Taiwan, New Zealand, and Istanbul I put my foot down. And in a moment of weakness I offered to hold the reception at our house.

Unless one is Queen Elizabeth and has matched place settings for hundreds in the kitchen cupboards, my advice would be to forget any ideas about having a wedding reception in the home. Our silverware consisted of a grouping that would serve perhaps three people in complete compatibility. The rest was a mixture of gifts or hand-me-downs, plastic and/or lost in the sand pile. Our best water goblets sported red-outlined silhouettes of various popular Walt Disney characters, and by squeezing in borrowed folding chairs and utilizing the bathtub we could seat about twenty-five people comfortably throughout the house. I told Lee we would definitely have to redecorate.

"Why?" he asked.

"Because you can't entertain wedding guests with chocolate syrup running down the dining room walls."

"Who is going to do all this redecorating?"

"Guess!"

"But you've let three weeks go by. We only have one left before the wedding. You should've said something sooner."

"We'll all help," I promised.

"Don't count on me," Karen announced. "I have to have my dress altered, my shoes dyed, plan a honeymoon, have a perm, go to a shower and bachelorette party, help Dave pick out a tie, and see that his brother doesn't back out at the last minute. I'm certainly going to be too busy to paint."

Susan, who intended to move into Karen's room the minute the last grain of rice was thrown, said, "Don't count on me. I have to measure for curtains, dust closet shelves, clean, shake rugs, throw away a lot of things, and call my friends and tell them I'm moving. I won't have time to paint."

John and David offered to help, but lasted only long enough to spill canary-yellow paint in the bedroom, turpentine on the stairway, and practice putting pop-top tabs on Augie's tail in case Dave's brother didn't show up and Augie had to carry the ring after all. Mary flounced around the house saying that as long as we were buying all this new stuff she could certainly use a canopy bed, and Amy and Claudia were thrilled with the sudden change in routine and the fact that no one remembered to tell them to take a bath. They were receiving new dresses, new shoes, and new underwear, and felt weddings were certainly worthwhile. Lee was in shock and I was tired. Not enough time and a grouchy husband is a rotten combination for anything, including interior decorating.

Dave said his mother was going through the same thing at their house preparing for the rehearsal dinner, and his dad was cross, too, and that he certainly hoped Karen wouldn't get that upset about entertaining after they were married. Karen laughed and said she probably would and Dave looked scared and doubtful, at which she burst into tears and said, "You don't love me." He said, "Yes, I do," and she called the whole thing off. It was two days before the wedding. Lee and I were still saying good morning and good night, but the stretches in between were pretty quiet.

Dave's mother and I decided since we had worked so hard we'd go ahead with our plans and hope the two of them showed up. "Augie will come," I assured her, "and Auntie-dear and I will be there."

It was a lovely wedding. Everyone was there, including the bride and groom but not the dog: Karen had put her foot down about that. Everyone said the right thing in the right places. I tried to forget that my hair was frosted with sea-mist green (the color of our living room) and flamingo pink (the color of our bathroom) and that it clashed with my dress. I knew that whatever I had forgotten on the lists was probably not important and it was too late to worry about it anyway. I relaxed and was sorry to see the ceremony end. Susan said I had dozed during "I Love You Truly," but I didn't think so. The reception went off without a hitch and not a soul noticed the father of the bride and the father of the groom sitting in the corner, behind the serving table, sharing three magnums of champagne and a bottle of Jack Daniels. At least, if they did, they were kind enough not to mention it. Our guests left and Karen and Dave departed for their honeymoon in a shower of rice and tears. "Isn't it wonderful," I told Lee as I perched on the side of the bathtub watching him try desperately to unplug the toilet. "How happy they will be."

"Don't count on it," Lee growled. "Some people don't know when they are well off." He had a plumber's snake wrapped around his neck and a cold towel on his head; Amy, Mary, and Claudia were standing in the doorway demanding immediate relief, and Augie, who was still spiffed because he hadn't been invited to the wedding, was barking constructive criticisms. I told him it wasn't my fault he had a headache from too much champagne and that I didn't know my sister was going to drop her glove in the stool and stuff it up. And he said most people didn't wear gloves when they went to the bathroom and if everyone would leave him alone he'd try to get the plumbing back into operation and that as far as he was concerned this was the last wedding he was ever going to attend, let alone pay for. I didn't think it a good time to remind him that he had four more daughters and two sons waiting in the matrimonial wing. I heard him complaining, but down deep I knew he didn't mean it. Not really. I sent the two little girls to the neighbors, the dog to the boys' room, and brewed some hot coffee for later on when he would need it most. How could anyone have romantic notions, I theorized, while playing the role of a human Johnny-mop? It had been a long day for all of us.

I wondered if Karen and Dave realized that marriage

had to survive the hard spots as well as the soft ones. Probably at that point they didn't know, or care, that eventually one of them could very well wake up some morning and have a deep-seated urge to heave a jelly doughnut in the face of the other. I wondered if they knew that to *think* about heaving anything was fine, but to actually heave it was big mistake.

"Should I call the kids and offer a little marital advice?" I mentioned casually to Lee as I leafed through the yellow pages for a plumber.

"I think they'll get more good out of the set of dishes we gave them," he said, foaming a little around the mouth as he retrieved a white glove, a dead sock, three toothbrushes, and a black crayon from the depths of the plumbing. He disappeared with a cold beer instead of hot coffee and found a quiet spot on the couch in the living room. I suppose he napped . . . to dream of carefree bachelor days when "Go fish" meant exactly that and not an afternoon of casting for gunk in the family potty while he had a hangover.

I was pretty sure Karen and Dave would find out for themselves that marriage is often like that. You have to take the plumbing with the poetry and ordinarily a couple doesn't find these things out until after they've been married a while.

No one had told me that Lee hated to answer the telephone, and no one had told him that I hadn't spoken a civil word before noon since I was fourteen months old. We went into marriage completely ignorant of these facts. We had to find them out by experience. The first time I peeled out of a soapy bath to answer the phone as it reached its ninth ring and found Lee casually reading the newspaper three feet away from the receiver, I had to make a quick decision. Did I pour shampoo in his ear or say, "Don't get up, sweetheart, I'll get it?" Somehow, I was smart enough to know my whole marriage could be hanging in the balance of one wrong number. Naturally, I answered the telephone. I am still doing it. And he accepted sipping orange juice across the table from a grump. Even the houseplants bow their leaves when I get up in the morning.

I am a night person. Lee is a day person. This happens occassionally when people marry without consulting the proper authorities . . . like parents or each other. Somehow mating gets all mixed up with genes and adrenalin and blood flow and things like that. When we were dating, Lee gallantly propped his eyelids open and danced until dawn, and I happily prepared a picnic breakfast and gaily met him in the park, smiling all the while. I didn't flinch when he invited me to watch a sunrise, and he didn't seem to care that I only reacted to artificial stimulation before 10 p.m. and became a veritable bundle of active joy after midnight.

However, twenty-nine days and four hours after signing our marriage license we had to arrive at a compromise in order to get some rest. "I can't stay up all night and hold down a job," Lee declared, his head bent wearily over the rhubarb surprise I had whipped up. It was 1:30 a.m. and he had been up since six that morning. "I get indigestion when I eat this late."

As the experts say, the honeymoon was definitely over. I had just polished off two glasses of milk, a peanut butter sandwich, and a raspberry tart, and was reaching for his portion of rhubarb. I was also getting ready to measure the kitchen for new wallpaper. I wanted to be a good wife, so I told him we'd do it his way. We went to bed at 9 p.m. At 9:01 I counted the tufts on our chenille bedspread, at 9:05 I went to the bathroom, at 9:10 I recited the Declaration of Independence sixty-seven times, at 9:15 I went to the bathroom, at 9:20 I heard burglars, and at 9:25 I went to the bathroom hoping to run into them in the hallway so I would have someone to talk to.

Oh, we worked it out. Lee has learned to cat-nap with his eyes open as we stay up at night. He smiles and nods appropriately when I go over the day's events with him. And I took over answering the alarm in the morning, and he allows me about fifteen minutes downstairs alone to punch out the coffee pot and shove eggshells down the disposal to work out my frustrations before he kisses me good morning. So alike are we now that sometimes I go to bed first and he grogs over breakfast.

I had only a few words of advice for Karen and Dave. "Don't sweat the little things . . . concentrate on the big one: each other." And I waited and waited for them to ask. They didn't, but I told them anyway. And added a few other things besides. As far as I'm concerned that's what a mother, and a mother-in-law, is for.

29

Guest Child
Is Always Welcome

The children remaining at home couldn't understand why we treated Karen and Dave with such dignity following their marriage and continued to behave so rottenly toward them. When the newlyweds returned home from their honeymoon, Lee and I looked upon them as guests.

"Boy," John pointed out, "how come you let old what's-his-name put his feet on the coffee table? I've never heard you tell him once that you're going to amputate *his* arches."

"Karen just comes over here and sits," Mary complained. "She doesn't have to help with dinner or clear the table or anything. You might as well make a red carpet and roll it out when they drive up in the driveway. It isn't fair." And with that she sat down and made out a list of potential boys who were in her grade at school and who might some day consider her as a bridal prospect. "I'm going to marry young so I'll be treated like a princess, too." She was twelve and I told her I wasn't going through another wedding for at least ten years, so she might as well stop looking right now.

"The other night," John continued, "Karen let the cat in and Dad turned a little red in the face but he only said, 'Now, dear, don't let the kitty in the house. The kitty lives outside in the strong, fresh air. It is good for him to be outdoors' and he reached down and petted the cat. All of us know he usually picks the cat up by its fur and tosses it out in the cedar trees. And cusses when he does, too." I remembered that incident and remembered the look on Karen's face. She had glanced around the room to see if she was in the right house. So did the cat. It stayed under Amy's bed for a week.

"I like to have them over," Claudia said, "Mommy doesn't yell and she makes dessert and I get to sit on Dave's lap."

"Oh, you're still little," Susan added. "Karen doesn't even talk to me anymore. She only looks at Dave with moon-eyes and holds his hand and talks about recipes and junk like that. She used to be fun." This entire conversation took place two weeks after the honeymoon. I rather enjoyed having a "guest-child." In fact, I had often dreamed of having a family that would come home and act like company. So it was with a great deal of pleasure that I saw Karen approach the house, knock quietly, and wait politely for me to unlock the door instead of pounding and kicking in the screen.

"Oh, I love your curtains," she commented graciously as she entered the house.

"Do come in and sit down," I invited.

She sat with both feet on the floor and didn't crumple in the chair like Kleenex and push the cushions into big wads. She had no sunflower seeds in her pocket to spit in the ashtrays and she didn't put her feet on the wall.

"Would you care for some iced tea?" I asked nicely.

"My yes," she answered courteously, offering to help if I would only show her where I kept the glasses.

"Please, don't bother," I said. "I'll get it. Do you take sugar?" I knew she didn't, but I thought I'd better ask to be polite. I put some delicate lemon cookies on my best tray and brought them into the living room. I was happy to notice that she didn't crunch ice with her teeth, spill tea on the carpet, or blow crumbs in the air.

Our conversation was extremely pleasant because it was give-and-take. It was not one-sided, and she didn't squirm and look miserable as I talked, but listened attentively and answered questions without my having to shout and flail my arms. And she didn't ask for money. She did bite her lip now and then, but other than that it was delightful.

She inquired about my health and didn't say, "Oh, you've got a headache—*again!*" and then expect me to prepare a fourteen-course meal in ten minutes. She was anxious about my condition and told me of some of the symptoms her mother-in-law had, and described a few of the home remedies she had sent along with Dave for their medicine cabinet. We talked about allergies and attitudes and she smiled softly while recalling that I had never allowed my children to be allergic because I didn't have time. She said she thought she might be developing hay fever and I clucked my tongue sympathetically and didn't say a word. She didn't grin and refer to my age when I complained about my inner workings not working, nor did she slap me on the back broadly and say heartily, "Well, Mom, you have to expect some of that when you get up there in age." She listened and nodded with compassion. Nor did she laugh hysterically and gasp, "Wait until Dad hears this one," when I described my latest automobile accident. She tsk-tsked appropriately and said, "Oh, that's too bad." I think she might have giggled a little because I saw her turn her head and cover her mouth, but I can't be positive about that.

It was a pleasant afternoon. She had been there fifteen minutes and it seemed like five hours. I was beginning to think "guest-child" was an awful bore, and she wasn't all that thrilled with "hostess-mother" either, I could tell. Lee came home from work and rumpled her hair and gave her a big bear-hug. He usually doesn't do that to guests, at least not in my presence. Karen seemed to like it, though, but quickly regained her composure and sat primly on the couch, not complaining when the boys brought home four of their friends to play soccer in the front yard. Why, only a few weeks before she would have been screaming, "Mother, make those boys stop peeking in my window."

Mary wanted to turn on the television and when I told her no she sat down beside Karen and asked her bluntly if Dave slept with his mouth open and I shushed her and indicated I didn't think that was any of her business and waited tensely for Karen to explode into one of her I-don't-know-why-I-have-to-put-up-with-this-kind-of-nonsense-in-my-own-house routines. Instead, she quietly patted Mary's shoulder, said, "Sweet child," and we talked about the weather. But I observed her clinched fists out of the corner of my eye.

The air was so thick with nervous strain you could cut it with a hacksaw. We sat there, the two of us, Karen yawning behind polite fingers and I having to go to the bathroom and not knowing how to excuse myself, when Susan wandered in from school. "Guest-child" sprang from her chair like she had been shot from a cannon.

"Do you see that!" she screamed. "She is wearing my good sweater. Mom, you promised you wouldn't let her wear my clothes, and there she is. I can't have anything around here. Lay something down, and—whoosh!—it's gone."

"What do you mean?" Susan screamed back. "No one told you that you could take my hot rollers on your dumb honeymoon, either."

"Those were halfies," Karen cried. "Half mine and half yours. Weren't they, Mom? Tell her they were."

I sat back and listened and their shrill voices settled over my shoulders like a fat, warm comforter. The boys had stopped playing outside and were standing in the door with smiles on their faces. Mary had turned on the television full blast and was watching cartoons with her chin in her hand, Amy had knocked over my iced tea and was drinking most of Karen's, and Claudia started to cry when Lee came up from the garage and demanded to know what the hell all the racket was about.

I jumped from my chair, clapped my hands, and said, "I'll make supper. Someone call Dave and tell him he is eating here tonight."

"I'll fix the gravy," Karen laughed happily.

"And I'll set the table," Susan said.

"I'm not going to do anything," Mary added dreamily. "I'm getting married soon."

Dave came in, put his feet on the coffee table, and I told him to take them off or not only would I remove his arches but snip off his toes. He grinned at Karen and said,

"Thank God, we're home!" and she said, "I'm so glad."
So was I. "Guest-child" was terribly dull, and besides, who
wants to be that polite all the time?

30

Mommy Takes a Trip

Ordinarily I wasn't given the opportunity to scamper off on little side trips without my husband and children. If I did go anywhere alone it was to the maternity ward of the hospital, and I always managed to pick up another family member within hours of checking in, so I don't think you can call that "alone." But it simply didn't occur to me to leave my family at home while I junketed off to spend time in a motel. I wasn't a martyr about it, because in our corner of the world none of the women I knew did it either. If they went anywhere by themselves, it was to spend a few days with their mothers, and since my mother had never invited me without her grandchildren I had never had the occasion, or the urge, to do even that. So when the chance came shortly after Karen's and Dave's wedding for me to attend a three-day PTA convention in a nearby city with my neighbor, Helen, naturally I hesitated.

Lee encouraged me to go. "It will do you good," he said eagerly. "We'll miss you, but I think we can survive." He rubbed his hands briskly together and started hauling out my suitcases.

"But I don't have to go for a month," I protested.

"Just wanted you to have everything handy," he said, "so you wouldn't change your mind." Helen said her husband Ray had done the same thing. She had even caught him waxing the round table in their kitchen and counting poker chips. "I think he's up to something," she said. I agreed with her. Every time I saw Lee and Ray together, they had their heads close and they were laughing to beat all.

The children were just as excited as their dad when they watched me pack. "Why aren't you taking Daddy's shaving kit?" Claudia wondered as she peered into my suitcase.

"Because I'm not taking Daddy." I had to grab her by the nape of the neck to keep her from running around the neighborhood yelling, "Divorce."

"Why are you taking your scissors?" Lee asked, as he saw me tuck the shears in the satin lining of our luggage.

"Because I'm staying in a motel room without you and I don't want to go unarmed. I'm afraid of guns and knives, but if any strange person walks in on me while I am sleeping I know how to handle scissors."

"You're being silly," he exclaimed. Easy for him to say—he was used to running off on business trips. It wasn't out of the ordinary for him to curl up in strange sheets alone (I had always hoped he was alone), and he could sleep through anything, even robbery and rape. But not me. I'm the nervous type and I had never had the chance to test the "Ms." in me before. His toothbrush had always been in there with mine. "Don't forget that Helen will be with you."

"She won't be any help. She's more high-strung than I am." Helen weighed about ninety-eight pounds and had confessed that the last time she had been on a trip out of town by herself was when she was eight years old and had taken a passenger train to visit a cousin thirty miles from her home town.

My hands were wet with sweat when we checked into the motel. I had to do it, because Helen absolutely refused to approach the desk. "What if he thinks we're call girls?" she trembled.

"I'd be flattered," I giggled. She gave me a dirty look and said maybe she should call Ray and have him come right down and get her this very minute if that was my attitude. I told her not to worry, nobody would ever think we were anything but what we were—stable, clean-cut members of the PTA community. She was wearing a prim navy blue basic with tatting around the collar and I had on a tweed pants suit with a turquoise lapel pin. We definitely didn't look like call girl material.

After registering, Helen was weak with relief because

the clerk had barely raised his head when I signed our names. I began to get over my disappointment at being totally ignored as we approached our motel room. We settled in and began to unpack. And we found out as we unpacked that we had brought much the same things. We both had sturdy flannel nightgowns, warm robes, and scuffy slippers. We had no nylon, net, or anything new— only the familiar, comfortable things we wore every day. I mentioned to Helen that I didn't think it was the typical motel attire, and she said she was glad we didn't have to impress each other with anything appetizing or inspirational. We agreed that it was rather relaxing.

I placed my scissors carefully on the bedside table and practiced grabbing for them as Helen checked our room for dust and to see if anyone had broken the paper strip on the bathroom stool. "If it's broken," she said, "I'm going to ring for maid service and make them fix it. Ray gets so mad when I do that. You won't, will you?"

"Heavens, no," I said. "You do what you want. You're a grown-up woman with brains."

"Isn't this fun?" Helen chuckled gleefully as she skipped about the room. "To know that someone else is going to make our bed, pick up towels, and clean the ashtrays no matter how much we mess things up? Look, I can drop this tissue on the carpet and let someone else pick it up. Just like the children do at home." I noticed a glassy look in her eye and thought for a minute she might toss the whole damn box on the floor, but natural instinct wouldn't let her. I had to admit it was a great idea to think about.

We toured the motel after unpacking. It was a tall, multi-floored building with several dining rooms, convention centers, and various recreation rooms. It had a red carpet and supposedly no surprises. Both of us laughingly confided that we were scared to death of elevators, and admitted that the only two things that might frighten us more were uninvited guests in our room and the fact I might not find my scissors in time.

The elevators in the motel were small, compact, and self-operating. We debated about even using them. But we didn't want to be constantly climbing up and down stairs every time we attended a workshop or wanted to eat.

"Don't be afraid," I assured Helen, "riding an elevator

is like having babies . . . everyone does it." She wasn't too convinced. But then she'd only had two babies to my seven. I told her she could take my word for it, and she did. She later said this was her second grave mistake. The first was coming with me at all.

For a while riding on the elevator was sort of fun. We whirred up and down, taking turns punching the buttons, and were always joined by others, making it a jolly crowd. Even Helen forgot to be scared.

We joined the convention group for a get-acquainted hour of coffee and doughnuts. The party was located in the basement, at what we thought was the bottom of the building. We milled through the crowd, stopping now and then to chat with a casual acquaintance and to munch on doughnuts. I must have eaten half a dozen to Helen's nibbling consumption of one, and then she complained of gas from overeating.

"I think I should go back to our room for some bicarbonate before the afternoon meeting," she said. "If you want to come along we could run hot water and use soap." Helen really knows how to live it up, I thought to myself, but agreed to go with her.

Stepping into the elevator, we discovered that this time we were alone—just the two of us and the control panel. "Surely we'll be all right," I soothed. "We've been using this particular elevator all morning and nothing has happened. I'll push the button and we'll whiz right up to our floor." But we didn't whiz—at least not up. When the door of the elevator opened we were facing a brick wall.

"My God," Helen screamed, "where have you taken us?"

"How would I know?" I spat back and banged the button again. The door shut and then opened again. We were still walled up solid. Where red carpet and a wide expanse of hallway had smiled before, there was nothing but thick, crusty bricks with no light showing through.

"We're stuck!" Helen shrieked. "Help! Help!"

"I know we're stuck, and be quiet. No one can hear you. Not from the bowels of hell. If we take this calmly and think, we can get out of this all in one piece."

"The air is going," Helen gasped, turning sheet-white. She was stiffening fast. Lord, I hadn't thought of that. Of course the air was going. I had seen that on television. It always happened.

"We are buried alive," I softly sighed, watching the elevator door continue to slide back and forth over brick. "No one will even know where we are."

"They'll miss us at the workshop," Helen said triumphantly, a splotch of red hope appearing on her pale cheeks.

"There will be four hundred people at that meeting. No one will ever know we are gone."

"Ray will miss me," she sniffled.

"Not until day after tomorrow, he won't," I reminded her, "and by that time it will be too late. We're goners, I'm afraid. Face it." She started to sob and my past flashed through my mind. It was extremely dull. "If I ever get out of this," I thought to myself, "I really must do something about that."

Helen interrupted my boring biography with a sudden idea. "Let me stand on top of you and push the tile away from the ceiling and climb out for help," she said, and with that she shoved me to the floor and threw all ninety-eight pounds of herself on top of my back.

"You're goring me," I cried out in pain. She had dug her high heels in my shoulder without giving my bones a second thought. "Please get down." I had no intention of letting her use me as a ladder to escape, leaving me all alone to die in a stupid elevator. I stood up, shrugged my shoulders, and she tumbled to the floor, tearing her tatting on my lapel pin as she went down.

"Now look what you've done," she whimpered, and she leaned on the brick with both hands and groaned out a throaty, "Help, help" The two of us stood and scratched on the brick wall for what seemed to be an eternity.

"I am going to push that button one more time," Helen said, baring her teeth, "and if it doesn't work I'm going over in the corner and do the last thing left to do . . . pray. I'll ask God to forgive you for what you've done." She gently ran her fingertips over the panel. We felt a shift and a rumble. The elevator was moving and we were blessedly going up, up, up. We landed on the top floor. We were free. When the door opened we flew out of the elevator and ran the six flights down to our room.

Back safely on my bed, I mumbled to my scissors, "Where were YOU when I needed you?" and Helen said she wanted a drink.

"But you don't drink. It bothers your stomach."

"Today I drink," she said. "The hell with my stomach." When we reached the bar she tossed down two gin and tonics like they were lemonade. We had walked to the darkened, empty cocktail lounge and surprised a bartender who wasn't used to having middle-aged, respectable PTA members frequent his joint at 10:30 a.m. "If old Ray could see me now," she giggled.

I reflected on our experience in the elevator. "You know," I said, "we really wanted out of there." Helen nodded in agreement. "Do you think it was because we were really scared or was it the fact we were stuck in the elevator with each other? I wonder," I said, looking her straight in her slightly blurry eyes, "how you would have reacted if Robert Redford had been in that elevator instead of me?"

Helen wouldn't admit to a thing. And neither would I.

31

Family Traditions

Anyone marrying into our family inherited not only a great many relatives but also had to become accustomed to the traditions that had been handed down through the years. Most of these had been started when the children were small and I established certain traditions as a change of pace. Lee went along with them and the children loved them. They stuck.

St. Patrick's Day was one of my favorites, even though I had no known forefathers from the Old Sod. I wore as much green as I could, always running the risk that I would be mistaken for a fat, sturdy celery stalk when I answered the door, and I dressed the children appropriately. I tried to get Lee to wear green socks, but he refused. "You'll get pinched," I warned, and he grinned optimistically.

I wasn't taking any chances that a leprechaun would leap from our chandelier and cast an evil spell because I was wearing a yellow blouse on March 17th. I had all the evil spells I could handle, right in my own kitchen, thank you, without having to worry about gnomes puttering around. Therefore, I celebrated St. Patrick's Day with a gusto that bordered on hysteria.

"Now what!" Lee protested when I set green pancakes before him for breakfast.

"Don't complain," I said. "They won't poison you, and the children like it. It's good for them . . . it's traditional. It gives them a grasp of history. A touch of their roots."

"We aren't Irish."

"We could be. At least I could be. We both know there are definite places on my family tree where the branches are barren. I've always thought some of my ancestors could have come from Ireland."

"Or Outer Space," Lee whispered into his coffee cup.

Augie-Doggie was the only one who absolutely refused to enter into the spirit of things. He refused green-tinted Gravy Train. He curled his tail in disgust and dug up the neighbor's iris bulbs and ate them. Every one of them. Our neighbor was furious and I told Augie he should be ashamed. He looked at me as if to say, What does the world expect from an animal that is cared for by a crazy woman?

I searched cookbooks for authentic Irish menus. Wanting to be a professional and factual, I considered cockles and mussels, alive-alive-o, but I didn't know what they were or where I could buy them in Nebraska. And when I got as far into the recipe as "fish them out of liquid and discard the empty top shell and the beard," I decided iris bulbs didn't sound bad. I wasn't going to cook anything that grew a beard, leprechauns or no leprechauns. Porridge sounded easy enough, but it reminded me more of Goldilocks than Paddy O'Grady. A dish called "Drisheens with Tansy Butter" had just the right ring to it until I saw a picture in full color. It resembled a blown-up bicycle tire, and in reality was made of sheep's blood served with melted butter. I could almost smell the iris bulbs simmering.

I settled on a traditional stew with Irish potatoes, tossed salad, and bright green baking powder biscuits with a surprise baked inside each one for good luck. Plain, nourishing, very Irish, and suspenseful. First I tried little plastic toys as the surprises, and tucked them in the biscuits, but they melted and ruined the dough the minute the oven heated up. I threw them away and started over. Eventually, I found the easiest thing was slipping small pieces of paper that carried a special message to each member of the family as well as a designated hiding place where they might find their St. Patrick's Day presents. I refused to fix Augie one because he was a bad sport.

Karen found a ceramic kitten she had been eyeing in a local gift shop, David and John discovered a regulation soccer ball to share, a charm for Susan's bracelet was in her jewelry box, there were new water colors for Amy, a book for Mary, and Claudia received Barbie doll clothes. The children were thrilled with the whole concept and thought I had created a terrific tradition. Even Lee was excited and bit into his biscuit eagerly. His slip of paper read, "Something you wanted. Something you love. Look under your pillow in the bedroom above." Swiftly he raced up the stairs, visions of golf shoes, a folding fly rod, or binoculars dancing in his head. With anticipation he reached under his pillow and found his prize—a picture of his wife. Did I see a slight flicker of disappointment cross his face? Of course not!

"Poor Daddy," Claudia said.

"What a gyp," echoed David.

"It's the luck of the Irish," I said happily. Kissing Lee soundly on top of the head, I promised to add a golf ball or two to the next year's green biscuit.

Naturally, some of the traditions changed as the children grew older, and although I stopped serving bilious-looking pancakes and surprise biscuits on St. Patrick's Day, I didn't stop wearing green. As far as I knew, that leprechaun was still hanging around somewhere just waiting to nip me when I least expected it.

And then came the year I told my family we were no longer going to spend the traditional millions of dollars for Christmas gifts. Lee's sigh of hope could be heard around the world. "We aren't going to overextend our credit or be caught up in the commercial world of fancy tinsels and glitters. We're going to have an old-fashioned Christmas."

"Does that mean you won't make that sour divinity anymore?" Claudia said hopefully.

"We're not giving up everything," I said over a chorus of groans that I tried to ignore. "But we are going to do something different. We're going to draw names, keep secrets, and make every single present."

"What do you mean, 'make'," John asked. "From a kit?"

"No kits," I said. "From scratch. Your pattern, your design, your originality. Your very own homemade product. I've been waiting for the day when you were all old enough to produce your own Christmas gifts."

"I hope whoever gets my name can throw together a

stereo," Amy said quietly. She had been licking the windows of music stores for weeks.

"I can't make anything," David confessed. "Do you remember that cedar chest I tried to make in industrial arts that ended up being a curio box? No one will want me to get their name."

He was right. No one did want him to get their name. They didn't want me to get their name, either. Lee made me promise, right before the children, that if I drew his I wouldn't sew his present on the sewing machine. He had to bring up the pair of boxer shorts I had made him for Valentine's Day when we were first married and the fact I had put the fly in backward. He said that was the most frustrating thing that had ever happened to him in his life and he never wanted to go through such trauma again. I promised not to sew anything but asked if I could knit it and he said no, just to make him some divinity and call it quits.

"This isn't going to be stuff you bake, is it?" John asked, pointing at Mary. "If she bakes fudge and gives it to me, I'm not eating one bite. She'll put Exlax in it for sure. You have to make her promise that if she gets my name she can't bake fudge."

"You don't bake fudge," Mary said, curling her lip, "and if I get your name I'll put it back anyway. I have no intention of making or buying you a present." She says that every year. And every year he's the first one she spends her money on, picking out just the right gift. That has become a family tradition, too.

"No, you won't throw away his name," I said firmly. "One of the rules includes keeping the name you draw. No growling, no throwing the name on the floor and stomping, and no trading. You can't trade names."

"Can I keep my own if I get it?" Claudia asked. "I'm going to send myself to Disneyland." I told her she couldn't keep her own name and if everyone took this in the spirit in which it was offered it could be the finest Christmas yet. One by one, they had to admit it might be exciting. "I'll make you a shotgun if you'll make me a motorcycle," David told John.

"Is Auntie-dear in on this?" Susan wondered out loud. "You know what she'll make. The only thing she can do is crochet doilies." I reassured her there was no reason to bother Auntie-dear and make her more nervous than she was already by adding the pressure of imagining what the boys would do if they opened up a package that contained a doily.

We drew names in late October, and secret fluffs began to appear in and out of the house. There was a hustle and bustle of glue, scraps of cloth, wood shavings, paint, screams of "Get out of here!", whispered conferences on the telephone, giggles, grunts, hammering, sewing, and varnishing. It seemed that everyone was producing something memorable for Christmas. Some were having an easier time of it than others. I served as consultant and had my fingers on the pulse of the entire operation. I nixed $595 worth of lumber ordered by David who was going to build a waterbed for his Dad; told Amy, though I knew Karen loved pretty things, I didn't think an ice sculpture would last through Christmas Eve; and I shook my head sternly at Lee, who was planning to hire his done.

Karen, who stood at the top of everyone's list as "The Person I Want To Get My Name" had her gift made, paid for, and gift-wrapped by November 1st; Susan said she'd probably wait until Christmas Eve to start hers, that she worked better under pressure; and our son-in-law admitted that his might be spotted with blood, maybe a few tears, as he wasn't all that handy. I told him it was the thought that counted and that I knew everyone would love their presents and that we'd all keep them forever, look back and say "Remember when?" and that this might be the most fun family tradition of all.

Every year I continued to hope that whoever gets my name can cut diamonds properly and with precision.

32

Sharing Ideas about
Marriage Can Cause Divorce

I felt it my sworn duty to share with Karen all I knew
about marriage. Gathering up all the odds and ends of my
wifely knowledge, I compiled them in a scrapbook and
offered it to her as an anniversary gift. "It's like an en-
cyclopedia," I explained, "only cheaper." She seemed impressed and thumbed through it with interest. Claudia
wanted to look at it, but I told her she was too young.
"Don't worry," I answered her, "I'll have one for you when
it's your time." Beth, who was soon-to-be-a-Lueth-bride,
thought she would like one for a wedding present.

"Is it a sex manual?" Mary asked. As a college junior
she had developed a frankness and candor that often
caused Auntie-dear to slump over in her chair and complain of shortness of breath.

"What's Mom know about sex?" John blushed. Although
he had graduated from the University of Nebraska, he still
thought his parents didn't do those things, had never done
them, and never would.

"The children are always the last to know," I grinned
at him, "but no, it isn't a sex manual." Mary lost interest
and left the room to search in the closets to see if Amy
had gotten any new clothes during her absence. "It's a
bit of information that I've gathered over the years to
make it easier for husbands and wives to live more har-
moniously."

"I'd sure like to see that scrapbook," Lee said, holding
out his hand.

"So would I!" Dave said with concern. Skirting the

issue, Karen cheerfully tucked the scrapbook out of sight and dashed into the kitchen to fix our lunch. I was beginning to think there wasn't one thing I could teach this daughter of ours. Nevertheless, there were probably one or two situations in there that she had not faced yet, and preparation is part of solving any problem. For instance, I wondered if she had faced . . . *The Income Tax Season* . . . or what I referred to every year as "The Poverty Period." During the months of January, February, and March, Lee carried a calculator around the house, checking cupboards, refrigerator, freezer, and garbage cans for empty noodle sacks, moldy leftovers, and lettuce leaves that could be salvaged. He didn't allow house lights to go on until it was pitch black outside, and I often cooked by the light of the flame on the stove, which was kept low to conserve gas. Long distance calls were severely restricted, and our conversations were sprinkled with words like assessments, dues, payments, donations, principal, assets, and liabilities . . . Lee always stressing liabilities and looking straight at me. It was tax season. It would be all over in April and we would live again. But until then he would sit around the house with his head in his hands, looking down at our checkbook and the W-2 forms, shoulders drooping, his shirt unraveling before my eyes, his hair growing down over his collar, wearing a suit coat that seemed to spring holes in both elbows. He was a true child of the depression.

For years, during this impoverished ninety-day period, I believed that if I bought one extra tube of toothpaste or indiscriminately scattered milk money to the children, burned the toast or wasted Kleenex, I would immediately plunge us into bankruptcy.

"Where does it all go?" he moaned, riffling through our monthly bills.

"I don't know, don't ask me—I haven't spent a cent." I ran to hide the White Sale bargains I had charged, only that day, under the bed. I didn't think it was a good time to tell him I had saved $11 on a $110 purchase. The percentage of savings didn't look half as good under the blinding light of my husband's inquisitions. It had looked darned good in the department store.

"Just look," he continued, with a scornful scrutiny of

our budget. "We spent hundreds of dollars eating out last year. Why don't I remember eating out that often? And there are ten or fifteen magazine subscriptions to pay for and not one damn magazine in the bathroom when I want something to read. Where *are* all of these magazines I'm expected to pay for? And right here it lists bolts and bolts of material . . . double-knits, Dacrons, India cloth, cotton, denim . . . hundreds and hundreds of dollars worth of material, and the sewing machine hasn't been used in months. Why do we have all of this spare cloth and no one sews?"

"I don't know, don't ask me. I haven't spent a cent," I laughed nervously, flying to call Helen to tell her we wouldn't be having dinner out with them on the weekend because I was expecting a bad cold—one that would probably last until after April 15th. And then quietly I warned the children that from now on if they needed nutrition pictures, funny animal faces, or drug articles for school they had to ask Auntie-dear for her magazines, because we wouldn't be having any for a while. The material I had stacked up in the utility closet I hid with the bed sheets.

"Aha!" Lee waved his pencil victoriously, a glow covering his face. "At least we can cut down on birthday presents. Not necessary, not necessary at all. That's where we can definitely save money." His calculator danced in pure ecstasy. I don't have to tell you who has a birthday during our poverty period, do I? Of course not. It is my birthday. My birthday is in March. His is in November, the day after we receive our Christmas Club check. I've always hated it that my birth date had to fall during our yearly recession, but as I wrote in Karen's advice book, when a person marries, no one promises her a rose garden *or* a birthday present.

The Hobby . . . My mother told me I should develop an interest in my husband's hobbies, so I did. I learned to fish, golf, and watch football without pouting. I threw my back out bowling and shot myself in the foot with a bow and arrow. He took up carving and I applauded and bought him soft walnut wood, and I allowed him to hang his paintings wherever he wanted in the house. But I often think fate plays tricks on those who don't live the way they should, and evidently I made someone mad because they came to collect one summer evening. Lee was sleeping soundly on the couch, Augie was sleeping soundly on the floor, the children were out-and-about, and I was virtually alone and unprotected, watching a rerun on television about a young mass murderer with a black beard, a mania for rock music, and the habit of attacking helpless middle-aged women while their households slept. A knock on our front door startled me, and when I opened it to a tall young man with a black beard, earphones on his head, cut-off jeans on his body, and as far as I was concerned, my personal ruin in his eyes, I felt my life was definitely over for all time. He held something in his left hand. A shotgun? A pickax? A rapier? There was no doubt about it, I was positive I would be ravished while my husband and my dog snored their little hearts out. I looked at the stranger carefully and I decided if I was going to be ravished, he wouldn't be a bad choice.

"Good evening," he said politely. "My name is . . ." I didn't catch his name because my heart was beating too loud. "I noticed your home. It looks old." He was certainly right about that. "I would like to use my metal detector to scan your lawn." His request sounded reasonable and I decided I was safe, as I had never heard of anyone being murdered by a metal detector. I was relieved that he wasn't carrying a weapon, but I woke Lee up just in case.

"There's something funny going on in our front yard," I whispered as I shook him awake. "I think you'd better get up." Possibly I should have let him sleep, for the minute he noticed the metal detector in the man's hand and the earphones on his head, it was like he was charged with electricity.

"My God, this is fascinating," Lee commented as he squatted down by the detector nosing its way over our lawn. "Why don't you join me in a beer" he said. "Let's talk about this hobby of yours." And that is how I became a pirate.

We soon became the owners of our very own personal metal detector, complete with one thousand dry cell batteries and a set of very cool earphones. Mind you, we could've bought a cute little rocking chair for the living room or a cute little winter coat for me or a whole lot of cute little groceries for the winter months to come. I tactfully outlined this to Lee.

"It will pay for itself," he told me. "Wait and see. Who knows what is buried beneath the ground waiting to be discovered?"

I will tell you what is down there. Grub worms. Millions of grub worms . . . ugly, ugly, grub worms that squeal when you cut their bodies in two with a digger.

"Grub worms don't squeal," Lee said, looking at me as if I had lost my mind. "Quit puckering your mouth up and probe." It was his job to man the detector, mine to unearth what it found. The children loved it. They followed him enthusiastically about the yard, waiting for the hum of a potential treasure beneath the earth.

"Maybe this is a silver ring," Mary said, rapidly scratching the ground with a long screwdriver.

"I could use an old Indian Head penny," David hoped, his knees in the dirt.

"Perhaps it's a treasure chest full of gold doubloons," Lee fantasized.

"In Nebraska?" I asked, but it wasn't long before I, too, became caught up in seeking and searching. Frankly, I wanted my share of any silver and gold that might be found. But I couldn't find anything. I dug and dug and dug. My fingernails became black-rimmed and broken to the quick.

"There's absolutely nothing down here," I insisted to Lee, after spending thirty minutes looking.

"But I'm still getting a reaction. There has to be something here. Keep trying," he would say, waving the metal detector in an arc in the general area of the crater I was digging.

"A minute ago I heard something say 'ouch.' I think I'm going too deep. I have probably hit China." Lee walked away and said I'd never get rich with that attitude.

In one month I found fourteen rusty nails, one hundred and ninety-five pull tabs, three 1979 pennies, a bolt, a belt buckle, and a hinge. But I was doing what my mother had told me to do and what I was suggesting our daughter do— joining in my husband's hobby. If it paid off in my fortune, so much the better. If not, I wrote in the scrapbook,

I still couldn't complain, since he often took me to dinner because I had been a good sport and introduced me to his friends as his best digger. It might not be gold, but it's worth its weight in something.

The Furnace . . . Turning to this page, I told Karen it was about games married people played and how she could win at them. I pointed out there were certain things she should look for when summer ended. Personally, I didn't have to look at a calendar to know that fall had arrived. I knew it was here because Lee and I started to fight over the furnace. He didn't feel it was economically feasible to turn on the heat before Thanksgiving, even if the temperature had dipped below freezing. He continued to assure me that it might seem cold in the early morning hours but the chances were great that it would be July-hot by late afternoon. "And then what would you do with all the heat stored up in the house?" he said, looking up from the newspaper in which he was studying the weather report carefully.

"I could turn on the air conditioner," I countered slyly. "In October!" he shouted. It was nearly more than he could bear. He almost stayed home from work that day so he could keep an eye on my finger. He was probably right, and it didn't really make sense to twirl heat off and on without thought—but that didn't help me when I was standing in the bathroom with my hand iced around a toothbrush.

"Keep moving around," Lee suggested, when I complained it was like brushing your teeth with the tip of an iceberg. "Get your blood circulating. You'll warm up."

The children huddled at the breakfast table, little faces turned toward the east, hoping to get some heat from the rising sun.

"If everyone dressed properly, half the battle would be won," Lee sighed. "The other half of the battle is state of mind. Think warm." He was wearing a large canvas hunting coat with down insulation and drinking his early morning coffee with mittened hands. I was wearing seersucker baby-dolls that had been washed one thousand six hundred and fifty-eight times and were cold to the touch. My eyes strayed toward the heat control located in the dining room.

"Don't touch the thermostat," he warned, pulling his muffler around his throat.

Did he really think I would resort to the furnace-flicking game right in the open where he could see? With nonchalance and a bit of deceit, I walked carelessly by the thermostat, ignoring it completely. Lee watched every move I made. I hummed quietly to myself and pretended to dust the dining room table with the tail of my baby-dolls.

"Don't touch the thermostat!"

Attempting to divert his attention long enough for me to flip the switch, I feigned being hot.

"Don't touch the thermostat!"

I opened the door for Augie, who came in shivering. He stood expectantly over the hot-air register. He felt nothing coming through the ducts but a draft. The poor dog was stunned, for it had been warmer outside. He ambled casually toward the heat control.

"Don't touch the thermostat!"

Newspapers rattled on the coffee table and sailed through the air as a chilly breeze blasted through the house. "Would someone please shut the door?" Lee begged.

"And waste all that good summer air!" I tossed my head in disbelief, and my hair made soft tinkling noises as the icicled tendrils clicked together.

Lee motioned me to his lap and encircled me in his arms, holding me close and folding me in his jacket. He whispered in my ear, "Is this better?" It certainly was.

"It's cold in here," John yelled. He was standing over the toaster warming his shoulders. "Why doesn't someone turn up the heat?"

"Don't touch that thermostat!" I said.

I know when I'm well off, and I hoped by reading the scrapbook and thoroughly digesting its contents, Karen would know when she was well off, too.

And then we became grandparents and scrapbooks became absolutely meaningless, irrelevant, and totally out of date.

GRANDMA WILL YOU BABY-SIT? NOT TONIGHT, THANK YOU

Grandchild Stage

33

At Home with the Angels

I had nearly forgotten how many Band-Aids a three-year-old needs. In fact, Band-Aids had almost become obsolete in our house, used only for razor cuts and an occasional paring knife slash. Scissors could be left out on the arm of the chair without worrying that someone would trim Augie's tail or a sister's head. The silverware drawer stayed reasonably neat, my ceramic figurines didn't run the daily risk of having their faces chewed off, diapers were turned into dust rags, and I no longer attended church services with spit-up on my Easter suit. The Christmas tree hadn't been knocked over in years. We were a household of grownups . . . or semigrownups . . . and we no longer paid seventy-five cents an hour for baby-sitters.

And then our first grandchild was born. I won't say trumpets sounded or bells rang, but I will say we welcomed her with a hug, sent her home with a kiss, and knew the in-betweens belonged to someone else. After twenty-odd years of inoculations, midnight water calls, stray puppies, traumatic trips to the dentist, stamping out seven thousand valentine cookies with a rusty cutter, and spending more time hovering over a potty chair than a cushiony love seat, I was a great believer in being a grandparent. In fact, as I told Lee, it was worth having children for.

I intended to be the Perfect Grandmother. I wouldn't meddle in our granddaughter's upbringing. I wouldn't cluck my tongue at Karen when she fed her carrots instead of the all-day sucker she cried for. Nor would I threaten Dave with an ear job when he scolded her for fiddling with the television knobs. She was their child, and

I would stay out of it. I had no intention of hinting that she was much better behaved when her parents weren't around. I just said so right out loud.

"That's because you let her do as she pleases," Karen said, grabbing little hands as the baby reached for America to strip her of her leaves. "If I had touched one of your plants, you would have made me stay in my room for a week."

"That rubber plant has outlived its usefulness," I said, pooh-poohing any idea that I might be granting special privileges to a grandchild. "It stands around sucking up good oxygen." Lee told me I shouldn't be so silly about being a grandmother and then spent thirty minutes talking to a stuffed bear because it made her giggle. In all of our married life he hadn't spent thirty straight minutes talking to me.

Being a grandparent wasn't hard, I decided, if you knew how to handle it. I learned to be calm while our grandchildren were in the house and how to collapse gracefully the minute they were gone. They seldom took naps, sat in high chairs, walked through the house, or cried. They quite often made mud pies, chewed on my good pearls, misplaced Grandfather's best pipe, went through my purse, lost car keys, gave crumby loves, and spilled milk.

"Why don't you turn into your 'madwoman of the kitchen' routine when *they* spill the milk?" Claudia asked as she watched me smilingly wipe up the mess our grandson had made. "Because he's little and doesn't know any better." A standard grandmotherly answer.

Now I had long leisurely days to myself to paint, to sew, to work in a flower garden, to read, watch television, chat on the telephone, and to do all those things I was never allowed to do with a clear conscience when our children were all small and still at home. No longer did the Baby Angel rattle his rattle, point a wet diaper at me, and say, "Shirley, dear, you need companionship. I will put you back into the swing of things. I have a spare baby here . . . I am going to give it to you." The Baby Angel concentrated on making me a grandmother instead. It was better that way. I wasn't astonishingly sick in the mornings nor did I have muscle cramps in my legs at night, but I could still look forward to having warmth and softness on my shoulder again and to have someone around who knew no four-letter words. I could buy our granddaughters open sandals in February, knowing I didn't have to hear them cry out to wear them when it was snowing, and get our grandson a tricycle, aware that he wasn't going to ram it into my good buffet. It was fun smelling baby powder in the bathroom instead of over-powering teen-age hair spray. And I knew I had a chance to correct some of the mistakes I might have made along the way with our own children.

"Go ahead, eat the worm," I told our grandson, know-ing that when and if he did it wouldn't hurt him and he'd still grow up to be six feet tall at the age of fifteen. He was the child I could take to the public swimming pool and have people think I was a nice old grandma, and both of us could get by with murder. I could cuddle and coo, buy jawbreakers, and turn my head when he tried to drown the kid next to him. I didn't apologize once to other mothers sitting there with their trim figures and dis-infectants. I settled back on my fat thighs, enjoyed myself, and knew they were all going to worry themselves into an early grave over trivia.

For Christmas and birthdays I gave our grandchildren turtles, finger paints, goldfish, drum sets, ant farms, bub-ble-blowing sets, real little oven-lovin' baking outfits, and miniature snow-cone machines and politely told them not to open their gifts until they got home so Mommy and Daddy could be surprised too. I didn't blush and want to drop dead when our granddaughter ate with her fingers at an expensive restaurant or our grandson blew his nose in his napkin. I let them eat ice cream as a main dish and french fries for dessert.

And I didn't promise one soul that I wouldn't squeal on their parents, either. There was nothing in writing that bound me from telling our grandchildren about the things their parents had done. There was no way I would go along with the myth that not once, in all of their chil-hood, had they ever given *their* parents one moment of distress. Therefore, with all of this grandmother-goodness in their background, I couldn't understand why Karen and Dave decided to move out-of-state and were taking two of our grandchildren with them.

"What have I done?" I asked Lee. "Why would they want to take them away? Did I do something wrong? Was I a bad grandma?"

"I don't think it had anything to do with you," Lee reassured me. "I think it had something to do with a job opportunity, a boost in their economic level, and a new experience."

"But so far away. Why do they have to take them so far away?"

"I don't think two hundred and fifty miles is considered the same as going to the moon."

"It is if you don't drive more than ten miles an hour on the interstate," I shot back. "Do you realize if I want to see them in the middle of the week and have to drive myself, it would take me nearly a month to get there?"

"You won't get there at all," David interrupted while buttering four pieces of bread, two sweet rolls, and a leftover piece of pie. "If you drive ten miles an hour on the interstate, you will be in jail." I couldn't see how he could eat anything while faced with this family tragedy.

"What if our grandchildren forget me?" I sniffled, a tear slopping down over my eyelid. "They could, you know, I've read stories like that."

"Oh, they won't forget you," Lee said soothingly. "I don't think anyone in this family will ever forget you."

"Amen!" David mumbled with his mouth full.

"John did when he went to college and met that girl. Remember? He didn't call home for a month. Not even for money." I sat down heavily in my rocking chair, overwhelmed with it all.

"He didn't forget," Lee smiled softly. "It just slipped his mind for a while. He had other things to think about."

"Amen!" added David, and I told him to brush up the crumbs and leave the room if he was going to talk like that.

I suppose I was silly to worry. They hadn't lived in the same town with us for years, but they had always been in the same state. We shared the same governor, paid the same taxes, rooted for the same football team, and if it snowed at our house it usually snowed at theirs. "They'll probably even talk different," I said, horrified with the thought of never being able to communicate with our babies again.

"People in South Dakota talk just like we do," Lee informed me with his I-am-getting-rather-tired-of-this-conversation tone of voice.

"Nevertheless," I said, "I must have done something wrong to make them pull up stakes and move—just like that—practically overnight."

"They've been talking about it for six months. Don't you ever listen?"

"Of course I listened, but I didn't think they were serious. I thought they were kidding. Do you think it had something to do with my cooking?" No one said anything, but I could've sworn I heard a faint "Amen" coming from another part of the house. I honestly thought our son-in-law had grown used to my cooking. He said he had developed a taste for funny stews and flat biscuits.

"I can't possibly be considered an interfering grandmother," I said, squaring my shoulders and my chins. "I don't take sides."

"But you put up No Spanking signs in the kitchen when any of them visit," Claudia said, tossing her long dark hair in disbelief.

"And I take them down when they leave," I reminded her sharply. "Well, I suppose I could look on the bright side. Karen said when they come to visit that they will have to stay at least three or four days to make the trip worthwhile." Lee looked a little taken aback at that. "And when I visit them I can stay two or three weeks."

David had wandered back into the room to rummage through the breadbox and said, "Boy, I'll bet old Dave never thought of that. I bet he would've turned down the job if he had."

"I'm a nice person to have come visit. You'll see someday when you marry and have your own home and I come to visit you. I'm sure they will be very happy to have me." And with that I closed the conversation. Why wouldn't they want me, I thought, mentally packing my bag for my first trip. I don't take up much closet space, I peel potatoes for supper, and I almost always bring presents. All I could say was I bet they would miss having my good close-by advice on child care, marriage problems, recipes, and budgeting the household finances. I had years of expert experience to offer them, and I bet they weren't going to find anyone in South Dakota to help them out like that.

34

Spoiling Grandchildren
Is a Fringe Benefit

The day eventually came when Lee and I were judged mature and capable enough to care for our grandchildren without their parent's supervision. Karen and Dave were going skiing for a weekend and with absolute doubt in their minds and with desperation in their souls they left Angie, who was seven, and Michelle, three, in our nervous hands. Susan and six-month-old Zackery were living in California at the time and Lee had to hold me back from the telephone to keep me from calling long distance and having him shipped C.O.D. so he, too, could take advantage of the weekend at "Grandma's House."

I prepared for days before their arrival (and recovered for weeks following their leaving) and Lee went to the grocery store for such staples as hot dogs, jelly beans, ABC soup, chocolate cookies with white centers to lick and rub on woodwork, plenty of pretzels, pancakes, and peanut butter. I had no intention of making them eat things like liver or peas or Cream of Wheat.

"Don't spoil them!" Karen said, drawing out a three-page composition of instructions. "Don't give them sweets between meals, please, even if they lay on the floor and kick, and you don't have to explain 'why' every two seconds unless you want to, and Michelle doesn't wear her 'dancing dress' to play in the dirt, and Angie only sleeps with three stuffed animals instead of the twenty-three she brought along and under no circumstances are they to sleep with Augie and the cat, I don't care how much they pout. Tell Dad he can say no in a very loud voice, and

mean it, if they tromp through his garden or pull up carrots, and Mom, you don't have to clean up their dinner
plate. Let them do it. And if they should occasionally
cry . . . let them. It will do them good."

For some good reason it had slipped Karen's mind that
I had once coped with all of these things without her advice. As had Lee. He said later, after they had gone, that
he thought for a minute Dave was going to tattoo their
names, addresses, and an emergency telephone number on
Angie and Michelle's little foreheads, just in case we became
careless and tossed them in the streets.

The next morning it took me from seven o'clock until
nine just to prepare a proper breakfast. I didn't have time
to dress them or myself so we were wandering around in
our night clothes and I was trying to fix them something
they would eat. Each time I set a conventional breakfast
dish in front of Michelle she said, "I don't eat that," and
shoved it in front of her grandfather. Lee had accumulated
four eggs—boiled, poached, fried, and almost raw—eight
strips of bacon, six pieces of jelly toast, three glasses of
orange jucie, two large mugs of milk, a doughnut, and a
bowl of snappy cereal.

"Mama said for us not to be picky," Angie said, gently
pushing her sausages in front of her grandfather, "but this
is icky, Grandma."

"What would you like to eat, Angie?" I asked kindly.
Amy, who had come through the kitchen on her way to
school, paused in the doorway, white-faced, waiting for
me to throw the dish towel and shout, "Get it yourself, if
you don't like my cooking." But I patiently waited for
Angie to make her decision.

"Oh, I think I would like a cheeseburger and Coke,"
she said, snuggling up to my shoulder.

"That would be fine," I patted. "How about you,
Michelle?"

"I like lunch meat," she said. "Mommy never gave me
lunch meat for breakfast before. I like it. I'll eat it, too,
Grandma."

"That's good enough for me," I said, shuffling to the
refrigerator to fill their orders. My bedroom slippers made
a slip-slap against the kitchen floor, causing Angie to giggle and spit her Coke on her grandfather. "Grandma

looks funny cooking in her nightgown," Angie apologized.

"Mommy never wore her nightgown to cook in before. Daddy won't let her," Michelle added.

"Well, your mother has never lived dangerously," I smiled, and jumped three feet as the doorbell rang. "My God, who's at the door at this hour?" It was Auntie-dear come to check on the girls to see if we were letting them run wild yet.

"I thought, my dear," she said, standing in the middle of the kitchen and glancing around with shocked eyes, "that you had outgrown this type of behavior and had become more organized." She looked at me in my nightgown like I was soliciting on a street corner instead of feeding grandchildren in my own home. "And what are these dear children eating for breakfast?" She peered over her trifocals at the banquet spread of cheeseburgers, Cokes, and lunch meat.

"Protein," I said, "lots of protein. It's good for them. They've had the flu. Their mother ordered it special."

"But Grandma," Michelle broke in, "Mommy has never let us . . ." I picked her up, holding her close and shutting her tiny mouth against my stomach.

"In fact," I continued, "it's time for their medicine right now. You can stay and watch if you like."

Karen had left nose drops and a cough medicine that tasted like cherry vodka. She also mentioned that Angie was good about taking it, but Michelle fought like a wildcat. I assured her I was no novice at dispensing medicine. Hadn't I poured gallons of expensive prescriptions down a million preschool throats in my day? It was all in how you approached it. With our own children I had just turned vicious, holding their noses and tossing it down, clutching them around the neck with a hammer lock. But grandmas don't do that, especially with Auntie-dear looking on, taking notes and preparing to report back to Karen the minute she arrived home. I used finesse.

"Now we will play doctor," I said to the two little girls, plopping them on the kitchen counter where I could reach them.

"But Grandma, Mommy said I was never to play doctor unless I checked with her first," Angie said seriously.

"It's all right, dear, Mommy won't mind if you play doctor with Grandma."

While Auntie-dear sat with hands folded and eyes staring, I tied a while dishtowel over my face, slipped garden gloves on my hands, and placed a barbecue apron over my nightgown. "Now," I explained, "Grandma is an important surgeon and I am going to cure you." I approached the counter with my hands held high in the air, shaking my fingers in a profesional way and growling deep in my throat with an "Open-wide, I want to check your tonsils" as I cavorted and clowned, oohing and ahhing, taking imaginary pulses, temperatures, and reflexes. The girls loved it. Angie said she was having the most fun and Michelle clapped her hands at the funny "Dr. Grandma." Lee said, "You've lost your mind, I'm going to work," and Auntie-dear seemed to be in a trance.

Sweeping up a clean teaspoon and the cough medicine, I reached the climax of my act. The girls were in the proper mood and eagerly waiting for the next step. "This is a cinch," I thought. "Who said giving medicine to little kids was hard?" With a majestic flourish and one last "ahhhhh-hhhhhaaaaa" I was ready to put medicine to mouth.

But I couldn't open the bottle. That hateful, adult-geared, child-proof lid wouldn't budge, not a squeak. It was like it had been soldered onto the bottle. Right before our grandchildren, Auntie-dear, and God, the good Grandma Doctor turned into the bad Grandma Doctor. No more make-believe. Throwing off the dish towel, gloves, and apron, I reverted to my rotten-tempered self. A self our granddaughters had never seen before. I'm not sure Auntie-dear had, either. "I cannot open this damn bottle!" I screamed.

Angie's eyes were like sunbursts and Michelle cowered behind her, whimpering, "I'll take my medicine, Grandma, I'll take my medicine." Auntie-dear had risen two inches off her chair. I pounded the bottle on the cabinet.

"I'll open it, Grandma," Angie said in a small voice. I slammed the bottle against the refrigerator door.

"I'll open it, Grandma."

I took the cap between my teeth and tugged. My bridgework loosened but the bottle cap didn't move an inch.

Michele was crying in earnest and Auntie-dear was nervously looking for her purse so she could leave.

"I'll open it, Grandma." Without another word I handed it to Angie, and she, with calm seven-year-old confidence, applied the right amount of pressure to the lid and turned. The lid slid off without spilling a drop and she handed it to me with a smile. At that moment . . . at that particular moment . . . she looked and acted just like her grandfather. I took a good belt of the cough medicine, gathered as much dignity as I could, and showed Auntie-dear the door.

After I promised cheeseburgers, lunch meat, and Cokes for breakfast as long as they were there, as well as no nosedrops at all, unless absolutely necessary, Angie and Michelle swore they wouldn't tell anyone that Grandma drank all the cough medicine and that we played hide-and-seek in our nightgowns, dressed and took a walk for ice cream, went to the park, and planned to have Grandpa take us all out to a fast-food hamburger place where they gave away pirate hats and diamond rings and that they could watch television until ten o'clock. We had a lovely day.

Their parents returned and forced us to give them up. I washed the fingerprints off the windows, put away the Raggedy Ann books, crayons, and tinker toys, and I looked longingly at the lunch meat in the refrigerator at breakfast time, trying to get Lee to try it . . . just once. I went back to my afternoon nap and lost four pounds because I was no longer eating their leftovers. Our ears became used to the silence.

But not quite. We missed them. I didn't want to say so out loud, just in case that Baby Angel might be listening and get some funny ideas. Once more for old time's sake was OK for some people, but I was quite content to remain just a grandmother.

35

Hiding Grandma's Wrinkles

"Do you realize," Lee said, sitting at his desk with a palm-sized calculator in his hand, "if each of our children have seven children we could end up with nearly fifty grandchildren?"

"Don't worry," I said, "we won't baby-sit them all at the same time." Not even I'm that devoted to grandmotherhood. His fingers continued to fly over the calculator keys. "And if each of them have seven, that's over three hundred great-grandchildren."

"Golly, my innovation of cheeseburgers, Coke, and lunch meat could make the family history books—a classic breakfast like that," I said thoughtfully, trying to decide if I wanted to include a picture of myself in my nightgown holding a mixing bowl and spoon or go with one in a strapless evening gown.

"Think of the Christmas list we'd have," he carried on, clicking figures like crazy, "If we spend, say, ten dollars minimum on each person, that's over three thousand five hundred and seventy dollars just for trifles and doesn't count the tree, cards, or any entertaining, not to mention friends, Auntie-dear, or birthdays. It's staggering."

The thought of spending over $3000 for Christmas thrilled me to my inner bones, but he looked so hurt and down-in-the-mouth I didn't want to mention it. Instead, I cheerfully told him that I didn't think we had to worry, because it wasn't fashionable or patriotic to have seven children in this day and age. "People look at me funny now when I admit to it," I said. "No, I don't think any of our children will have that many." He looked so relieved that he put his calculator away and we went into the kitchen and had cold chicken and a beer to celebrate.

I didn't fall into the grandmotherly role overnight, nor did I fall gracefully. My mental picture of a grandma dated back to the one I carried of my own, who spent most of her time waiting on Grandpa and picking chickens. She definitely didn't eat them or drink beer at three o'clock in the afternoon. She went to church, weddings, funerals, and family reunions, and a weekly trip to the closest town on Saturday night for groceries was a highlight.

"Will I have to give up playing bridge now that I'm a grandmother?" I asked my friend Helen. She wasn't a grandmother herself, but she was smart about a lot of things, if you didn't count elevators.

"Well," she said, "you know that it is hard for some men to imagine a romantic relationship with a grandmother. Lee might start having second thoughts about your marriage."

"Our anniversary is coming up soon, and he's always been very good about remembering that. In fact, he says he'll never forget it. Maybe I should do something about making this anniversary memorable. Keep our marriage exciting. I don't want him to think just because I'm a grandmother I'm no longer interested in other things," and I winked at Helen, hoping she'd catch my meaning.

"Try Saran Wrap," she said, winking back.

"I don't understand." Her answer puzzled me. I didn't know what Saran Wrap had to do with making our anniversary memorable. "I don't want to preserve a casserole, I want to preserve my marriage."

"It's simple," she said with a strange smile on her face. She didn't look like the shy, backward, thin Helen I had grown to know and sometimes love. "I read in this book that a wife can add years of excitement to her marriage if she will occasionally do the unexpected. It suggested she remove all of her clothing, wrap herself in Saran Wrap and greet her husband at the door when he comes home from a hard day's work at the office. A strategically placed red bow is optional." Her eyes glittered and tiny flecks of foam appeared around her mouth.

"My God," I yelled at her, "I can't do that!"

"How do you know until you've tried?" she answered

221

calmly, picking at her nails like she hadn't mentioned anything more important than adding more soy sauce to the chop suey. I didn't have any idea that thoughts like that ran through her head. I wondered if good old Ray knew about this. I decided he didn't, he didn't really seem that happy to me. I reminded Helen that for one thing, it would take my entire monthly food allowance to buy enough Saran Wrap to cover the territory, and for another, the stuff was see-through.

"You're only making this difficult. It doesn't have to be. You have to toss down the gauntlet some time, and it might as well be wrapped prettily."

"I can't for the life of me understand how it would enhance our marriage if I met Lee at the door looking like a giant leftover. He'd laugh. I know he would."

"He might not. You're anticipating."

"He'd either laugh or throw up. I know him. Would aluminum foil work? I'd feel so much better in foil. It's not so transparent."

"No," she said, "I'm afraid foil wouldn't work. You'd scare him to death. I think it has to be Saran Wrap or nothing. It's supposed to be more intoxicating than champagne or red roses."

I could hardly believe what I was hearing. How could I look alluring air-tighting my pores in Saran Wrap? "What happens when I sweat? You know it clings. I'm sure I'd sweat. What did the book say about sweating?"

"Not a thing. It didn't mention sweat. Love books never mention sweat, you know that." No, I didn't, for I had never read one. "You're making this so difficult, when it really isn't. I know what I read and I'm passing it on to a good friend. If you don't want to take my advice, don't. Anyway, it worked for this lady. I don't know what it will do for you. If you want to know the truth, I think your marriage is in real trouble." She left in a huff. Maybe she was going to roll herself up good and tight and meet good old Ray at the door, for all I knew.

"I won't have to worry about it for a while, anyway," I thought. "I'll worry about it when our anniversary really gets here." I decided not to ask Lee's opinion. I'd surprise him when the time came. But I did have to worry about getting caught up in the grandmother syndrome whether

I wanted to or not. I didn't want to walk down the street and have everyone look and say, "There goes a grandma, I can tell by the way she walks and talks and dresses. I wanted them to say, "Who? You? A grandmother? I can't believe it," and appear shocked.

One of my problems was my wardrobe. I knew that, and ruffling through the clothes hanging in my closet it was obvious I didn't have the proper things to wear. Everything screamed, "Grandmother is wearing this pants suit. Grandmother is walking around in this blouse. Only a grandmother would wear checks." I called Helen to see if she was over her pout and asked her if she'd like to go shopping.

"Are you going to the grocery store?" she said triumphantly. "How many boxes are you going to get?" She sounded disappointed when I told her I was buying clothes. She agreed to come along only because, she confided, Ray had cut off her credit cards and if she couldn't buy, at least she could watch and give advice.

As we entered the department store she suggested maybe I could surprise Lee by buying something really different. "Like a ball gown," she said.

"I've never been to a ball in my life and you known it. What would I do with a ball gown? Besides, aren't they expensive?"

"Not necessarily," she answered enthusiastically, warming up to her subject. "I read this article that said according to fashion dictators we women no longer had to worry about where our next ball gown was coming from or how much it cost. They said we could wear our nightgowns and go right out dancing, straight from the bedroom."

In awe of this woman who read far too much for her own good—or mine—I took her arm and stopped in the center aisle. "You can't be serious," I whispered. In my heart I knew I had made a big mistake by asking her to come along with me.

"Naturally, I'm serious. I don't kid about things like this. It said that you could pluck your nightie right out from under your pillow and *voila!* off to the ball."

"I wear granny gowns," I told her. "I don't even think a corsage would help a granny gown look like a ball dress."

"Don't be difficult," she said, taking my arm and pulling

me toward the lingerie department. "It has to be something that flutters and looks transparent." There she goes with that Saran Wrap bit again, I thought, wishing I could become invisible.

"But Helen," I said in a no-nonsense voice, "you know Lee wouldn't go anywhere with me if I wore a nightgown."

"It won't hurt to look," she said as she tossed a pair of lounging pajamas that were bright red, shiny satin culottes tied below the knees with big bows to me. "Try it on. It's something you can sleep or samba in."

"Forget it," I said. I wasn't wearing culottes, and that was that.

"Can I help you?" a saleslady asked, coming quietly up beside me. She was older than I was, grayer than I was, and dressed tightly in a chin-up corset. She looked enough like Auntie-dear to give me cold chills.

"I guess I would like a nightgown," I stuttered. Looking very efficient and capable she pulled three or four serviceable crisp polyester blends from the rack and dangled them before my eyes. I was ready to buy all four and get the hell out, when Helen slapped her hands together and said, "No, no. These are nice, but she wants something translucent enough to wear with a body stocking. She wants to wear it to the next PTA cakewalk." And turning to me she said with a superior air, "Let's be realistic, dear, you aren't going to a ball." The clerk muttered that it was against her lifetime sales law to commit such an injustice and stood by helplessly as Helen pawed through the night wear hanging before us. She spied a slinky off-the-shoulder salmon-colored gown with one shoulder that tied with a shoestring bow. I told her I couldn't wear it because I would have to draw the bow up so tight in order to keep the gown on that it would cut off my circulation. She looked at a black nylon satin tricot with spaghetti straps. "My stretch marks will show if I wear a neckline that low," I pointed out. Helen brought out a tantalizing "teddy," but it only came in a size nine, thank God, and was a few hundred inches too small. She settled on a caftan with long sleeves, no waistline, and an unrevealing scoop neckline. Sighing, she said "we'll take it." The saleslady's corset rose two inches in relief. I didn't argue, for even I had to admit this was a perfectly decent piece of night wear, even for a ball.

"Isn't this fun?" Helen said, skipping along beside me. "Now we'll buy a dress. You have to have a smart dress."

"I haven't worn a dress in five years," I told her. "I haven't even owned a dress in five years, and quite frankly I don't want one. I am well pleased with the fact that I can get all dressed up *and* hide my legs."

"Nevertheless," Helen declared, "dresses are in." I followed meekly behind her, clutching my caftan. "I'll sit here in this comfortable chair while you try on a few dresses," she said. "I won't even pick them out for you this time. Do your own choosing."

I took five dresses at random in my size, or approximately my size, and stepped into a dressing room with a very small curtain. As I peered into the five-way mirror, I tried to decide if my rather unique body was a pear or a rectangle or a box. I decided it was definitely a rectangular pear-in-a-box. The fluorescent lights made my skin sallow and my teeth yellow. "Why don't they put candles in here?" I muttered between colored teeth. I tried on an outfit with the layered look. It was like Raggedy Ann out for a walk. Dumping that, I slipped on a classic black, one-piece crepe with tender tucks and delicate details.

"Let me see," Helen shouted. "Come on out and let me see."

"I look like a stork!" I complained as I stepped from the dressing room. "A black stork in heat." Helen laughed right out loud. I certainly didn't like the way things were turning out. It was supposed to be my fun shopping trip. Instead, there she sat, stretched out in great comfort in a brown overstuffed chair, chewing on peppermints while I was drawing attention to myself by parading around like a stupid stork.

"And I'm shrinking," I told her. "Just look. I'm shrinking."

"Well, stand up straight," she ordered. "Why are you all hunched over that way? Why are you walking with your knees bent?"

"Because I have on knee-length hose and they have runs. I forgot to wear pantyhose." That's what I liked about wearing pants suits. I could wear any kind of socks I wanted.

"I really am shrinking, Helen," I persisted. I could definitely see that I was inches shorter. Helen continued to laugh.

"What will poor Lee think when he wakes up some morning and has to hunt for me and finds me curled up at the foot of the bed . . . a tiny, shrunken woman who used to be five foot six-and-a-half."

Exasperated, Helen handed me a lovely deep purple, silken two-piece soft overblouse-type dress that was very stylish, very beautiful, and very expensive. "Here, try this one." I disappeared into the cubicle of footlights, sticking my tongue out at the mirrors. "This time," I told my reflections, "this time, I have found MY dress. This dress will make me willowy and thin and very, very tall." I was very, very wrong. I looked like a juicy, plump plum. An expensive juicy, plump plum. Standing on tippy-toe I stretched my arms to the ceiling. It didn't help. Nothing helped. There was no way possible that I could make that dress look as if it was made for me.

"Let me see," Helen called from the depths of her chair. "Come on out!"

"Not on your life. If you think I'm coming out looking like a fat fruit, you're crazy."

"Then I'm coming in."

"No, no!" I screamed, cowering behind the curtain, the mirrors flashing my image. I could hear Helen choking on her peppermints as she peeped in and viewed five roly-poly plums passing in parade. I snickered myself.

Grandly, I swept aside the curtains and stepped stoutly among the dresses displayed until I found something that I felt was womanly, dignified, and me. And I didn't care if I looked like a grandmother or not. I told Helen to sit in that chair, be quiet, and not to say one more word. I went back among the mirrors to try on a light tan, straight-lined dress, perfect for my coloring, my contours, and my age. It fit perfectly, the mirrors applauded, I smoothed down my hair, and said, "I'll take it." And I did. Helen tried to talk me into buying a fringed fuschia bolero to add dash as we left the store, but I told her to mind her own business.

Later, when I modeled my new caftan and dress for Lee, he was quite pleased and told me I looked very nice, even if I was a grandmother. Somehow, this made me feel younger and it was good to know that not only did the man I married have twenty-twenty vision but also great taste.

There was absolutely no doubt about that.

36

Hot and Cold
Running Hobbies

"Now that we are grandparents we'd better develop some interests," I told Lee. "Retirement is just around the corner and we don't want to be left watching the world go by."

"I won't be retiring for another fifteen or twenty years," he said. "Don't put me in the rocking chair yet."

"Well, I'm going to be prepared. You do as you like." I was determined to acquire a new skill. I bought a beginner's crochet book and decided to make great and wondrous and creative things. The book said that after mastering basic stitches I could spend many pleasurable hours making a variety of items. Bright colorful illustrations fell from the pages . . . a hairpin-lace afghan, a tank top, a sleeveless V-neck sweater, warm cozy slippers, and mittens . . . why, I could start making Christmas presents in May. By December I could whip up enough sweaters for everyone in the family, including the grandchildren, not to mention the shawls, scarves, and potholders I could throw in for good measure.

"I will save money, too," I told Lee. "I can buy the yarn on sale, and a crochet hook is certainly cheap. All I need are three fingers, and who knows what I can accomplish?"

He didn't get excited. He sat in his chair with the funny, crooked look he gets on his face when he knows something is going to cost him more money than he can afford. I'll show him, I said to myself as I settled down in a soothing spot in the living room with a brand new

tote bag full of hooks and things and announced to anyone who cared to listen that if little children in 4-H
learned to crochet, surely I could teach myself. Well, I
couldn't. With all my heart I tried to start a foundation
stitch and with all my heart I tried to get the thread to
stay together and with all my heart I tried not to poke the
crochet hook into the lamp shade. I kicked the tote bag,
and hot pink yarn plummeted onto the living room floor.
The cat was hysterical with joy. Augie had settled nearby,
out of reach of the hook, but near enough to see what
happened next. All human family members had left the
house. I bit my lip and single-crocheted the first three
fingers into the potholder I was trying to make. "I could
be a walking hot pad the rest of my life," I said desperately, as I tried to untangle the mess from tips of fingers
that were quickly turning blue. Augie covered his face
with his paws. He likes excitement but he can only take
so much. I picked up my tote bag, threw it against the
wall, and went over to Helen's for coffee and a piece of
sunshine cake. "I'm a failure," I admitted. "I can't
crochet."

She suggested that I take lessons. She said that she
had, and she knew the instructor. They were old friends,
and because of that she would make her take me in the
class. "She owes me one," she said, and went right to
the telephone to call her. She didn't tell her how unco-
ordinated I was and I was accepted into the class, sight
unseen.

The class was a group of fourteen ladies, forty skeins
of pretty yarn, and one patient instructor. It took me three
sessions to learn how to properly hold the hook, and by
that time one member of this beginner's class had made
a sweater, one had mastered the technique of broomstick
lace, one was well on her way to winning a purple rib-
bon at the county fair, one had single-crocheted a bedspread, and one was considering opening a hobby shop in
her home. The instructor started avoiding me along about
the fifth lesson. She didn't fool me. I knew she had seen
me waving my scissors, and I had definitely apologized for
bending my number G hook on her forehead the night she
stooped down to help me yarn-over.

I started to make a crew neck pullover sweater for

Michelle. "A grandmother should be able to crochet something for a granddaughter," I decided, and turned out a garment that would fit a medium-sized mouse. I'd thought the instructions that read "dc" meant decrease, as I had learned they did in knitting. My instructor shouted from across the room, "Dc means double-crochet! Double-crochet! Anyone can double-crochet!" I couldn't, so I had just skipped the lines that said that.

My second attempt was obviously made for the little crooked man who lived in a little crooked house and had crooked little arms. The sides were uneven and one arm measured fourteen inches and the other five. "It's not coming out right," I told my instructor, and she said any ninny could see that and ripped that sweater apart so hard and so fast the yarn fuzzed. Finally, after ten weeks of desperate concentration and sore fingers, I created one front (oblong), one back (square), and two sleeves (horizontal and perpendicular). I had a sweater. Eureka! It didn't fit Michelle and she cried when I tried it on her and didn't stop until I had fed her some lunch meat and promised that she didn't have to wear Grandma's sweater if she didn't want to. When I received my certificate of graduation in the mail that read "Shirley Lueth has satisfactorily completed the course in Crocheting I." I was so excited that I started picking out what I would wear to the alumni meeting. I even invited Lee to go along.

"I probably won't have time," he said. "I'll be too busy with my new hobby. I thought it over and decided that you were right." Boy, that was a switch. He never had come right out and said that before. "A hobby sounds fine . . . and I've chosen one." He had a mischievous light in his eyes, and for an old man he looked pretty thrilled. I couldn't wait to hear. Probably something practical like checkers, or horseshoes, or woodworking. "It's wood, all right," he snorted. "I am going to build a hot tub!"

All I could say was, "Why?"

"Because it's the newest thing in sophisticated circles," he explained. "Men and women bathe in it for relaxation. They're in all the magazines and it's supposed to be the perfect thing for people who are getting up there in age and suffering from arthritis, bursitis, and headaches." He knew I had all three. I told him my 1930s upbringing hadn't prepared me for bathing with strangers.

"You don't bathe with strangers, silly, you ask friends over to share it with you."

"Can you imagine inviting Helen and Ray over on a Friday night to take a bath?"

"It might beat bridge," he said.

"But they wouldn't come. And even if they did I wouldn't have enough nice towels to go around."

"You're missing the point."

"I can't understand it. How in the world would you serve refreshments with everyone splashing around?"

"I don't think anyone would care for refreshments."

"You know how Helen is. I couldn't invite her over without at least serving crackers and cheese. She'd tell everyone in town. And think what a mess all those crumbs would make. They might even gum up the plumbing."

"You aren't suposed to eat in a bathtub."

"I know that, but I'm not going to have people telling everyone how cheap we are. We *have* to feed them. And if all we're going to do is sit around in a bathtub with no clothes on it's going to be very difficult to plan a proper menu."

Lee just smiled.

"How would I invite them over for a bath, anyway?" I asked him. "I would think they would be insulted. I know I would be."

"I think it would be best just to call up and ask them."

"What would I say? I just put in a fresh load of water and bought some new soap, why don't you drop over and get clean?"

"I think that would do it," Lee grinned.

"What would I do with my eyes? My God, I'd have to look! I'd hate that."

"You'd get used to it after a while," Lee said confidently.

"No, I wouldn't. I never would. And neither would you." But by the way his nose was twitching and one eyebrow stood straight up, I wasn't so sure. Maybe he wouldn't have such a hard time, after all.

"Bathing with your friends is supposed to relieve you of the tensions of the day," Lee informed me.

"It would make me have a nervous breakdown," I said.

"It sounds like a darn good way to unwind to me. Warm water, good friends, stimulating conversation . . ."

"Tell me this," I said pointing my finger at his twitching nostrils, "What would we talk about, the weather? The children? Recipes? Water temperatures? Bathtub rings? Mid-section wrinkles?"

"Try ordinary, everyday conversation. You could handle that, you've had enough practice."

"I'd laugh. We wouldn't have a friend left."

"Why would you laugh at someone taking a bath?" he questioned.

"Think about it," I said. "Think about Helen and good old Ray and what they must look like sitting at home in their own bathtub and then think about having to sit there, looking them in the eye and trying not to notice things. Think about it. I'd laugh. I know I would." A small smile began to flicker across his face. I think he was thinking about it.

"Anyway, we should practice before you invest the money in building it and the only thing we have to practice with is our own bathtub and it's too small for entertaining, especially if you want to stick grownups in it. I've squeezed in three preschoolers and maybe added a first grader or two, but there definitely isn't room for us to crawl in with any of our friends."

He looked disappointed. I thought he had accepted my point of view. Then he left the room and didn't come back. I went to look for him, as I was going to cheer him up by telling him I had thought of a hobby we could do as a couple, and found him scrambling around in our bathtub with a tape measure. I think he was planning a party.

"Forget the hot tub," I said, "I have just the thing for us to do together."

His interest perked up and he started toward the bedroom. "Not that," I said. "We'll put in a communal garden. You and I. We'll dig it, plant it, harvest it, and preserve it." We had always had a garden, but it had been a one-man effort until now. His. He was surprised that I was even interested. "But you've never wanted to work in the garden before."

"I've never been approached to take a bath with people before, either. I feel gardening is much more grandmotherly than sitting in a bathtub with your neighbors. I think I might like it, and I could use the exercise."

"If we're going to do it right and do it together, you'll have to start from the beginning."

"I'm willing," I said, before he could change his mind. "I'll do anything you say."

"We'll start with the rototiller. You do half and I'll do half. You first."

Until that moment I had only a nodding acquaintance with the rototiller. I saw it when I entered the garage and I often said good morning and noticed its green teeth, but not once had I ever had a desire to see how it worked. We were content, the rototiller and I, to remain strangers. But Lee insisted, since this was a two-sided deal, that I had to do my part, and the rototiller was part of my part.

"You'll have to wait until I change my clothes," I said.

"You don't have to dress up to rototill. Wear what you have on. It looks fine."

"I'm not rototilling in a T-shirt!" I said. "Not for you or the neighbors or anyone to watch." He wasn't trapping me. T-shirts were fine for loading a dishwasher, but not for a very full-grown woman like me to shimmy in behind a jumpy rototiller. I'd seen how those things rock-and-rolled around the yard.

Realizing I had suggested this whole project, I approached the rototiller with a willingness to do my best. I didn't even become irritated when Lee discovered I was spilling gasoline all over the ground instead of into the machine and began shouting. "Pour it in the hole, not on the ground." I smiled, steadying my shaking hand. I am desperately afraid of gasoline. I was afraid I would breath too much of it or that it would explode or that I would acidentally spill some on my arm and burn my skin off. But I was a good sport. I didn't quit.

Family gathered from every corner of our house to watch. Karen and Dave came from out of town. The grandchildren sat quietly on the lawn and were given cookies to keep calm. John called from the West Coast where he was working. He only wanted to listen for a while, he said. "I haven't heard her yell for a long time. It will be almost as good as being home for the day."

I continued to smile, and prepared to move the rototiller to the designated garden spot by the side of the house. I didn't quit. Lee offered to help, but I bravely shrugged him off. I was independent and was going to do my share.

"That is one heavy son-of-a-gun," I muttered under my breath. But I didn't quit. I pulled and pushed and strained and struggled. It wouldn't budge from the garage. "How can I make it work if I can't move it out of the garage?" I wasn't smiling now, but I hadn't quit.

"I told you I'd help," Lee said. "I'll move it and take it where you want it." His muscles rippled in the sunlight as he easily tugged it across the lawn. Mine withered under my smock.

"What now?" I asked when Lee placed the rototiller where I wanted it. "What do I do now?"

"Start the motor," he said.

"How?"

"Put the gear in neutral, stroke the casement, shove the transaxle, adjust the automation, reverse the differential, and pull up the starter. It's easy."

I did what he said and nothing happened.

"Yank!" Lee hollered at the top of his voice. I yanked. My arm loosened at the socket but nothing happened to the rototiller.

"Pull! Pull! Pull!" he howled. I pulled and pulled and pulled. Nothing. Lee reached over, tapped the string gently with his little finger, and the rototiller lurched with a powerful shudder, heaved its mechanical guts into a pounding roar, and rumbled over the lawn . . . straight at our son-in-law.

He screamed. Karen screamed. Our granddaughters screamed, "Daddy, Daddy, run, run, run. Grandma is going to kill you!" And I screamed too. Louder than anyone. I also hung on for dear life, my feet drilling into the soil. I was being corkscrewed right through to the bottom of the earth. Buried alive by a rototiller.

"Stop!" came a large voice from the rear. It was Lee chasing behind me, puffing and panting, his rippling muscles reduced to mush. "You're attacking the neighbor's peonies." Wasn't that better than attacking our son-in-law? I thought so.

"Control that thing," Lee ordered. "Right now! You're ruining the driveway." In stunned disbelief he added, "Don't hit the car!" But it was too late. With a crashing crunch the rototiller and I removed the front fender of our car. The murderous machine stopped, and so did I. Turning calmly around, I looked at the crater I had created, looked in front of me at the car I had nearly destroyed, looked sideways at the grandchildren I had nearly robbed of a father, dropped slowly to my knees, turned off the motor, announced to the rototiller, my husband, my family and the world . . . I Quit! And I did.

All I can say is, give me my grandmother's day when girl babies were taught to crochet at birth, everyone bathed alone on Saturday night, and all it took to till the soil was a friendly burro, a little hand plow, a hitch, and a hee-haw and the garden was hoed.

In the good old days no iron-toothed monster tried to grab your foot off, and as far as I know, they didn't have hobbies, either.

37

The End?
Why, It's Only
the Beginning

In the past thirty years I've discovered there are few requirements for becoming a mother. I didn't have to take a quiz, renew a license, know how to spell, lose weight, sing on key, or be able to cook. I just did it. More often than most women, but not as often as some. And I'm sure most mothers would agree with me that if the stork had been thinking, he would've included a recipe for chocolate chip cookies with the birth certificate, along with a good quick cure for impetigo and heartache, two diseases that are bound to show up in a family where there are children.

A mother has a natural-born talent that takes root the minute she hears her baby's first cry. It covers a wide range of emotion and feeling. It's a talent that mystifies husbands, amazes small children, amuses some ministers, astounds doctors, and confuses teen-agers. The only people who don't think it's queer are grandmothers. You can't barter for it, beg for it, or buy it with money, and no mother worth her safety pins would be without it or use it indiscriminately. It's called "instinct."

It is invaluable in order to measure a little baby's 3 a.m. crying jag, a preschooler's awful nightmare, an eight-year-old's plea for "Just one more glass of water, please, Mommy," or a senior high son's footsteps in the hallway after curfew. A mother's instinct is especially keen after midnight. In fact, she knows if and when it is advisable or expedient to wake Father so he can share in the experience of providing room service to little children, a tongue-lashing to a teen-ager, or a manly hug for a son who needs a dad to talk to. This is when instinct and a poke in the back go hand in hand.

Who else but an instinctive mother can pray for peace and quiet in her home and then worry when she gets it? The silence of children doing nothing alerts a mother faster than the slam of a cookie jar lid. She knows that the hush of a household could possibly mean her good pair of pantyhose has been turned into circus tights, the master bedroom is being redecorated in bright red lipstick, the cat is taking a death trip in the dryer, the baby of the family is being force-fed two pounds of jelly beans by an older sister, or Daddy has just lost his priceless coin collection to the Ice Cream Man. When a mother complains of noisy children, she usually doesn't mean it.

A child's facial expressions are a dead give-away to an instinctive mother. Don't tell her an infant's first fluttery smile is gas. She knows better. She knows no one smiles when they have gas, not even a baby, and that nearly everyone smiles at Mommy. And instinctively, Mother tucks that smile away in her own memory bank to bring out during the growing-up years, when the smiles don't come as fast as they once did.

A six-year-old hasn't got a chance with those darned instincts. A mother knows when he's snitched his first bubble gum. It hasn't got a thing to do with jaw movements or saliva count. And the maternal X-ray vision can see inside a twelve-year-old's digestive tract and tell when a stomachache is being faked in order to miss a day of school, and sometimes, when her instinct says it's OK, she lets him get by with it, knowing a day spent cuddled up on the couch with a warm blanket, a soft pillow, and Mother's attention can do more for a child's intellectual and emotional growth than a day full of fractions and facts.

And woe to the teen-ager who thinks he is outwitting a mother. Not a chance. That's when the spy system works at its fullest capacity. Once in a while, maybe, when the instinct is tired, and so is Mother, she can be fooled into complacency, but it won't last. Let them be warned.

When it's really important, that instinct will get them every time.

A college education doesn't make anyone exempt. Mom is probably the first one to suspect that when a feminine voice answers a son's telephone, the new roommate might not be Joe, after all, but Joan, and she'll know the proper time to tell Dad. Trust her. And when the ad in the school newspaper appears listing for sale "graduation typewriter—used two weeks," it means book money has been lost again. And when no one comes home for three months because they are "studying," she hides her tears and doesn't tell Dad that she didn't think that is the real reason.

A daughter doesn't really have to worry, because she will inherit that instinct the minute she becomes a mother. As for sons, their wives will have it, so they don't need it . . . except to lean on now and then.

Eventually almost every mother becomes a grandmother, and that is when things begin to fall in place. That is when the instinct can fade away and almost be forgotten. Oh, it's still there. It has only changed faces. It's become what it was all along.

Just plain love!

Isn't it wonderful?